The Globa Vegan Waffle Cookbook

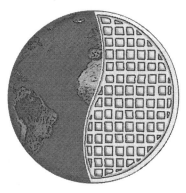

82 Dairy-Free, Egg-Free Recipes for Waffles & Toppings, Including Gluten-Free, Easy, Exotic, Sweet, Spicy, & Savory

Dave Wheitner

DIVERGENT
DRUMMER

First Paperback Edition
Divergent Drummer Publications
Pittsburgh, Pennsylvania

ISBN: 978-0-9817764-3-9

Library of Congress Control Number: 2010934428

Related merchandise: http://WaffleParty.com
Book feedback and inquiries, including special sales: pubinfo@divergentdrummer.com
Speaking and workshop inquiries: http://WaffleParty.com, pubinfo@divergentdrummer.com

Divergent Drummer Publications
Pittsburgh, Pennsylvania

Version 1.1

Contents

"GF" indicates gluten-free waffles. All toppings are GF, assuming use of wheat-free soy sauce.

Acknowledgments _____ *9*

Introduction _____ *10*

Cooking Essentials _____ *14*

Measuring & Timing Conventions _____ 15

General Vegan Waffle Baking Tips _____ 17

Yeast-Raised Waffle Tips _____ 21

Vegan Waffle Pantry Staples _____ 22

Waffle Irons & Other Essential Equipment _____ 30

Neutral Waffles _____ *36*

Naked Vegan Waffles_____ 37

Tropically Tanned Naked Waffles _____ 38

Mapley Waffles (GF) _____ 39

Nice Rice-Teff Waffles (GF) _____ 40

Textured Rice Waffles (GF) _____ 41

Yeast-Raised Waffles _____ 42

Sweet Yeast-Raised Waffles _____ 43

Pass the Buckwheat-Oat Waffles _____ 44

Heartfelt Banana-Spelt Waffles _____ 45

Yeast-Raised Buckwheat Waffles (GF) _____ 46

Buckwheat-Molasses Waffles (GF)_____ 47

Crunchy Steel City Waffles (GF) _____ 48

Crispy Cornbuck Waffles (GF)_____ 49

Flavory-Sweet Waffles _____ *50*

Original Cinnamon-Raisin Waffles _____ 51

Yeast-Raised Cinnamon-Raisin Waffles 52

Generously Ginger-Lemon-Chocolate Waffles 54

Banana-Blueberry-Teff Waffles (GF) 55

Crispy Maple-Cashew Waffles (GF) 56

Dark Chocolate Cake Waffles 57

Hot Chocolate-Molasses Waffles 58

Coconut-Date Waffles (GF) 59

PBMax (Peanut Butter to the Max) Waffles 60

Cider-Pecan Waffles 61

Cider-Banana-Raisin Waffles (GF) 62

Sinful Cheesecakey Waffles 63

Chocolate-Raspberry Cheesecakey Waffles 64

Chai Spice Waffles 65

Almond-Amaranth Waffles 66

Cashew-Carob-Molasses Waffles (GF) 67

Espresso-Key Lime Waffles 68

Mango-Chili Waffles 69

Orange-Ginger Snap Waffles 70

Anise Biscotti Waffles 71

Flavory-Savory Waffles 72

Spicy Blue Tortilla Chip Waffles 73

Carrot-Ginger-Sage Waffles 74

Spicy Carrot-Raisin Waffles 75

Orange-Basil-Cornmeal Waffles 76

Cheddar Cheesy Waffles 77

Refried Bean & Cornmeal Waffles 78

Refried Bean, Rice, & Cornmeal Waffles (GF) 79

Banana-Fofana-Walnut Waffles 80

Umami Mama Waffles: The Mother of Savory 81

Caramelized Onion & Garlic Waffles _____ 83

Chili-Lime Felafel Waffles _____ 85

Spanakowafflita _____ 86

Kale-idoscopic Waffles _____ 88

Avocado-Pecan Waffles for Two _____ 90

Yeast-Raised Cornmeal Chili-Dippin' Waffles _____ 91

Quinoa-Full Keen Waffles _____ 92

Keen Zucchini-Dill Waffles _____ 94

Some Awesome Samosa Waffles _____ 95

Mucho Molassesey Vegan Power Waffles (GF) _____ 97

Sesame Waffles _____ 98

Flavory-Sweet Waffle Toppings (all GF) _____ *100*

Dark Chocolate Syrup & Variations _____ 101

Crazeee Carob Syrup _____ 102

Banana-Maple-Nut Syrup _____ 102

Cocoa or Carob Agave Nectar _____ 103

Espresso-Maple-Walnut Syrup _____ 104

Maple Syrup Supreme _____ 104

Coco Kah-banana Syrup _____ 105

Very Coconutty Syrup _____ 106

Lemon-Ginger Drizzle _____ 106

Raspberry-Avocado Cream _____ 107

Cinnamon Cream Cheese _____ 108

Creamy Maple-Chai Dream Sauce _____ 109

Creamy Spiced Apple Pie Sauce _____ 110

Simple Piña Colada-ish Topping _____ 110

Amazing Amaretto Sauce _____ 111

Carob Halvah Spread _____ 111

Mexican Chocolate Ice Cream _____ 112

Mango-Vanilla Ice Cream _____ 113

Basil-Orange Ice Cream_____ 114

Flavory-Savory Waffle Toppings (all GF) _____ 116

Savory Cashew-Mushroom Sauce _____ 117

Coconut-Cashew-Basil Sauce _____ 118

Cilantro-Lime Tahini Sauce _____ 118

You Make Miso Tangy Dipping Sauce _____ 119

Mint Raita _____ 120

Black Bean-Mango Tango _____ 121

Southwestern Beans & Greens _____ 122

Spicy Sloppy Tofu & Portabella _____ 124

Southern Fried Tofu & Waffles_____ 126

Kalamata Olive & Sun-dried Tomato Hummus _____ 128

Ideas for Ultra-Quick Toppings _____ 129

*Organizing & Hosting a Waffle Party*_____ 130

What is a Waffle Party? _____ 131

Why an Event Featuring Vegan Waffles? _____ 131

History of the Waffle Party _____ 132

Developing a Vision _____ 133

Food Preparation Tips _____ 135

Vegan Party Etiquette _____ 139

Physical Setting Logistics_____ 142

Keeping It Environmentally Friendly_____ 144

Other Fun Ideas _____ 145

Inaugural Global Vegan Waffle Party Hosts & Cities _____ 146

Glossary of Waffle Vernacular _____ 148

Express Yourself _____ 149

About the Author _____ 150

*Index*_____ 151

This book is dedicated to a healthy, compassionate, and sustainable future for all of us.

Acknowledgments

My wonderful partner Jen provided support, encouragement, and feedback while I was completing this project, and selflessly tasted countless vegan waffles. Jo Stepaniak supplied expert feedback and motivation, inspired a few flavor combinations, and blazed the trail for vegan cookbooks such as this one. The Pittsburgh Vegan Meetup group, annual Waffle Party attendees, and Vegetarian Summerfest crowd shared inspiration and knowledge. Rich Bjork assisted with proofing and inspired some creative concepts via his pastry chef wisdom. The vegan blogging community has helped to spread word about this concept, as have the hosts of vegan waffle parties in other cities and countries. They have also boosted my energy to complete this project.

The waffle recipe test team volunteers provided detailed feedback and suggestions that impacted the text in multiple ways: Sallie Crick, Alice Doolittle and Tim Pearce, Emma Follender, Dani and Nir Goldman, Ida Hammer and Noah Lewis, Lauralee and Chris Holtz, Marty Kinnard, Heather Schall-Lucas and Alan Lucas, Benjamin Palmer, Anna Roberge, Ginny Silhanek, Rachael and Ron Smart, Sally Stewart, Stephy Tang, Patrick Thompson, Lisa Tirmenstein, Joanne Watral, Portia Wu and Brad Peniston, and Christine "Peanut" Vardaros.

Vance Lehmkuhl kindly produced the current Global Vegan Waffle Party logo. Gary Crouth snapped the bio photo during one of our parties. Thanks to David Bennett and Isa Chandra Moskowitz for additional ideas on chopsticks. Isa and Terry's cupcake creativity increased my confidence that vegan waffles can also catalyze positive change. Hillary Rettig provided additional perspective on authoring and publishing. Pat Clark unknowingly catalyzed my first "blatantly vegan breakfast" experience, and Robbie Ali inspired me to question the status quo in new ways. Our neighbors and the Pittsburgh Cohousing Group sparked further thinking on how diet fits into sustainability. My parents and family sowed the seeds of caring, justice, compassion, and creative experimentation that have evolved into my current understanding of the world. Thanks to our feline companion LeMew for helping to anchor the stacks of notes on the kitchen table. And of course, my deepest gratitude to the higher energy that joins all of us on this journey, however you may perceive it.

Introduction

Welcome to the first cookbook devoted entirely to vegan waffles and waffle toppings. A great addition to the experienced chef's collection, it is also well-suited for anyone just getting into baking. Whether you're practicing or merely exploring veganism, simply find vegan waffles interesting, or maintain a dairy-free or egg-free diet for other reasons, you'll find food here that hits the spot.

You will have the opportunity to enjoy a broad range of ingredients, and to incorporate flavors where you may not be used to seeing them. For example, have you ever seen kale or basil in a waffle? Non-wheat flours are included in many recipes, with more than a dozen gluten-free (indicated with "GF") waffles provided. Recipes range from simple to complex, from sweet to savory, and from traditional to avant-garde. The index includes recipes listed under specific flour types, under individual herbs and spices, and within categories including "gluten-free" and "yeast-raised."

To support you in your vegan waffling adventures, there is also a broad range of baking pointers specific to vegan waffles. These include descriptions of many of the ingredients and how they behave, troubleshooting techniques for quality issues, and guidance on selecting cooking equipment.

Once you've baked a few batches for yourself and your closest friends, you may wish to entertain even more. Perhaps you'll even want to leverage the vegan waffle as a mechanism of social change. The later sections include tips for planning and throwing vegan waffle events, including participation in the growing Global Vegan Waffle Party phenomenon. After all, it's not just about baking waffles—it's about creating a kinder, more sustainable world.

People choose vegetarian and vegan lifestyles for many reasons, including physical and mental health, environmental sustainability, human rights, animal rights, spirituality, economic justice, and reduction of global conflict. Each of us has a different set of values, priorities, and experiences. Some people begin to alter their lifestyles rapidly after a particular learning experience, while others take years as they obtain and process new information. As we open up to new data, and question what we had automatically accepted as truth, we often discover new and refreshing ways of living.

Growing up in a community where hunting and fishing were common pastimes, I had never considered the idea of living without consuming flesh and other products taken from animals. Seeing other living creatures injured, bleeding, and killed usually gave me a slightly ill feeling, but I believed that eating them was absolutely necessary—a part of our nature. Coincidentally, an 8th-grade science project titled "What Do Plants Need to Make Food?" took me all the way to Ohio State Science Day. I was already planting seeds for later life work, but I still had a few more dots to connect.

My first opportunity to spend a significant amount of time with vegetarians or vegans was during a 3,800-mile bicycle trip for a charitable cause. Our team of 25 cyclists had a limited budget for food, and I often felt annoyed when the vegetarians seemed to hinder buying more "real" food like hamburgers and sandwich meat. I didn't bother to notice that the vegetarians were riding just as many miles as the rest of us, without keeling over from lack of protein or other deficiencies. At the same time, I often felt somewhat guilty while eating around them, even though they never directly commented on my eating habits.

I later worked on a large environmental public health research project, with a medical doctor who had been vegan for decades. I was surprised that someone with an extensive background in medicine and public health would maintain such a lifestyle. He didn't talk about it much, but politely answered my questions. Doing my own research, I learned more about the impacts of animal product consumption, and I soon began to change my food choices.

I initially adopted an ovo-lacto vegetarian diet, giving up meat but increasing consumption of milk, cheese, and eggs. I mistakenly thought the latter were necessary for protein and other nutrition. Upon attending my first North American Vegetarian Society conference (Vegetarian Summerfest), I was surprised to hear so much discussion about veganism. My thoughts raced: "But isn't being vegetarian good enough? I've already taken this large step, and now I feel guilty all over again! This is becoming too difficult, and these people are annoying me."

However, the information made a lot of sense, even though I did not want to hear it at first. After further research, I began to see that animal products were not only unnecessary, but potentially harmful to my health. Although this contradicted most of what I had previously been taught, I considered the various epidemics associated with the standard American diet: heart disease, type II diabetes, obesity, cancers, and so on. I recalled how my uncle had died from a heart attack, and how my father had undergone bypass surgery at a relatively young age. I wanted to reduce my chances of suffering the same fate.

Only after changing my behavior was I able to look more seriously at the less selfish benefits of a plant-based lifestyle, such as the animal rights impacts, environmental impacts, and so on. When I had still been eating products taken from the bodies of other animals, I had felt too guilty and ashamed to consider this in any depth. Who wants to imagine the suffering of a dairy cow while enjoying a slice of their favorite cheese?

Soon recognizing that food was only a piece of the picture, I began to eliminate or vastly reduce animal products in other areas of my life. Because I still have room for improvement, I sometimes call myself a total vegetarian approaching veganism. However, the "perfect vegan" is a myth that makes veganism seem unattainable, and that discourages many people from making any changes at all. Also, it's not about earning a label; it's about continuous, incremental self-reflection and improvement to create a better world.

In the area of food alone, there's still much work to do, so that we can sustain the well-being of our planet, our health, and other living things. This is particularly in the realm of baked goods, most of which do not require eggs or dairy of any kind. I hope that vegan waffles, along with the vegan food parties described later, help to underscore this point.

When we mentally and emotionally detach ourselves during the intimate experience of eating, we deny our connectedness to our world in a very profound way. This has deep psychological and spiritual implications, because we may generalize this habit, and it may impact our ability to relate to others. If you or someone you care about has ever been the victim of racism, sexism, homophobia, or xenophobia, consider that these attitudes often include a sense of detachment or disconnectedness, and a "they're lesser than me" justification. This is similar to the attitudes that often accompany consumption of other sentient, living beings. Is this mere coincidence? All of us—humans and other animals—are in this together.

In addition to helping you create and enjoy a variety of vegan waffles, I hope that this book provides you and your friends with a deeper sense of connection, and increases your sense of fulfillment and integrity. Never underestimate the awesome power of a delicious vegan waffle.

Cooking Essentials

Overall, basic waffle batters and waffle iron technology are relatively simple, and most people with a desire to cook can make a waffle. Creating exceptionally good or fairly complex waffles, however, does require some knowledge, proper technique, and tools. This section will help you to understand some of the language used in this book, avoid some common pitfalls, stock your kitchen with the proper equipment and ingredients, and even improvise a bit when necessary.

Measuring & Timing Conventions

These are some of the techniques used in creating the recipes; following them will help to ensure that you enjoy similar results.

Measurement of flour

Do not sift flour prior to measuring or forcefully pack it into the measuring cup. Simply scoop it from the flour container with a measuring cup, or spoon or pour it into the measuring cup. Level the top by scraping off any excess with the flat edge of a butter knife.

Measurement of brown sugar

Because brown sugar is naturally moist, pack it into the measuring spoon or cup, and level the top with the flat edge of a butter knife.

"Packed" ingredients

This term most often appears alongside green leafy vegetables and herbs, including kale, spinach, and mint. It means to compress the ingredient into the measuring cup to remove most of the empty space, yielding a greater amount.

Measuring batter to pour onto the waffle iron

Each model of waffle iron has a slightly different surface area and depth, and some batters expand more than others. Thus, as a general rule, the directions recommend covering no more than two-thirds of the iron's surface with the first waffle, and adjusting the amount as necessary for subsequent waffles. The first time you make each recipe, you may wish to write down how much batter is required for your iron. You might use an actual measuring cup to determine this, or you might note roughly how much you filled your favorite ladle to get the ideal waffle.

Determining cooking time

Because different waffle iron models bake at different temperatures, the recommended time provided in each set of directions is approximate, and any recipe will require a small amount of trial and error with the first waffle or two. Even if your iron has a temperature adjustment knob, a setting of "5" on one model may not correspond to the same temperature as a "5" on another. If your iron has a built-in audio timer or "done" light, you may find that it is right on the mark for some recipes, but early or late for others. For these reasons, you may wish to utilize a standalone cooking timer or stopwatch (see page 33), and record the optimal cooking time the first time you try each recipe.

If you still have the owner's manual for your waffle iron, also note any manufacturer's recommendations such as required preheating time. Just be aware that any suggested average cooking times may have been generated using non-vegan waffles without fillings. Vegan waffles and waffles with fillings may require different baking times than other waffles.

General Vegan Waffle Baking Tips

Following are troubleshooting pointers to help you climb the stairway to Waffle Nirvana.

If waffles are tough or rubbery

You may have overstirred the batter after adding the wet ingredients to the dry ingredients. Where directions note to "mix just until blended," the batter should still contain small lumps. These lumps don't need to be any larger than the size of a standard chocolate chip. If they're too much larger, the finished waffle may contain dry clumps. Never use an electric mixer to mix the batter; do it manually with a spatula, spoon, fork, or chopsticks (if it's a yeast-raised batter).

Overstirring isn't as much of a concern with yeast-raised waffle batters. They require relatively vigorous mixing to break up the yeast-raised portion when it's blended with the liquid ingredients added later.

If waffles have clumps of dry flour

You may have understirred the batter, leaving clumps too large to absorb moisture. Again, don't be tempted to use an electric mixer; it just needs a bit more manual stirring. It's also possible that the batter didn't sit long enough. Where instructions note that a batter must sit for a specific period of time before baking, it's often because some grains and flours take longer to absorb moisture. Two examples are spelt and rice flour. These recipes often call for a second brief stirring prior to baking, which helps to break up any large clumps.

If waffles stick to the iron

If the waffles stick to the iron despite the waffles binding well (i.e., the iron is very hard to open), first make sure you've allowed adequate time for the iron to heat before each waffle. The batter should begin to sizzle as soon as it touches the surface, and some irons need a few moments to reestablish full temperature between waffles.

Secondly, make sure you're oiling both grills prior to each waffle, and using a consistently effective method to do so. This must be done even with a "non-stick" waffle iron and a batter containing oil, and it is particularly important with gluten-free waffles, spelt-based waffles, and those that incorporate ground flaxseed as a binder. I've had the best results with a pressurized spray can of canola oil or other cooking oil. For a round iron 7 inches in diameter, I spray each grid for a total of 1 to 2 seconds, making 6 to 8 quick sweeps across each grill in a zigzag pattern to cover the whole surface. It may be helpful to utter, "I love ve-gan waf-fles" as you spray, with a single sweep happening on each syllable. You may eventually find that your favorite waffles don't need this much oil, but this is a good place to start.

As with any pressurized item, just be careful not to leave the can sitting right next to the heated waffle iron. It is now relatively easy to find these cans without harmful chlorofluorocarbons (CFCs). While refillable oil spray bottles eliminate additional waste, I find that they don't generate a fine enough and even enough spray for waffle irons. I also don't recommend applying oil with a brush, as a few recipe testers reported this method to yield inconsistent results with vegan waffles.

If the sticking seems to be due to the waffles not binding well enough (i.e., the waffles easily split into top and bottom halves when you open the iron), let the next one cook a little longer before opening the iron, alongside spraying the grills with oil a bit more thoroughly. Some vegan waffles need a little longer to cook than non-vegan waffles. You may need to add 1 to 2 minutes to the time recommended in the waffle iron's directions, or to the "ready alarm" programmed into some waffle irons. This is particularly the case if the waffle contains fillings that hold moisture, such as chopped vegetables or fruit pieces. The first time you cook a particular waffle, you may wish to use a timer and jot down your preferred cooking time next to the recipe. This will reduce future guesswork.

If you're baking a yeast-raised waffle, double-check that you allowed the yeast to rise for at least the minimal suggested time, and that you used a non-metal bowl. Failure to follow these guidelines may result in a thinner, less-developed batter that's also more likely to cling to the iron.

Batters incorporating flaxseed as a binder can develop a greater tendency to stick if the batter sits for an extended period, and adding liquid may or may not resolve the issue. Generally, batters should be baked within half an hour of preparing them. When preparing the wet and dry portions of a batter in advance for a large event (see "Food Preparation Tips," page 135), leave out the flaxseed until the portions are combined shortly before baking.

If the above suggestions do not help, you may need a higher-wattage waffle iron. If your waffle iron is very old, it's possible that the coating has pits and scratches, especially if the grills have been cleaned with abrasive or metal items. Rather than metal forks or knives, use wooden utensils like chopsticks to lift out waffles and clean out "stuck" waffle pieces—even then, scraping too hard can damage the surface. And, of course, avoid plastic utensils as they may melt and create a terrible mess.

If waffles aren't crispy enough

Begin by choosing a recipe whose description includes crispiness, as some recipes yield crispier waffles than others. Then turn up your iron's heat if it is adjustable. If the recipe calls for standard sugar, consider experimenting with a darker sweetener such as brown sugar or molasses. Try increasing the amount of sweetener by 1 or 2 tablespoons. Just keep in mind that such changes are experiments, and may sometimes result in sticking or other issues.

If waffles are too soft or mushy

Whenever possible, serve waffles within 1 to 2 minutes of baking them, especially if they're yeast-raised. Otherwise they tend to get somewhat "floppy" as they sit and cool, and you may need to put them back in the iron or toaster briefly before serving.

If the waffles seem too soft right after coming out of the iron, you may need to cook each waffle a little longer. If the iron has an adjustable heat setting, try lowering it a bit to keep the exterior from burning before the inside has baked. Otherwise, when you try the recipe again, decrease the nondairy milk or water by 1 or 2 tablespoons, or increase the flour by 1 or 2 tablespoons.

If waffles are too dry

Add 1 or 2 tablespoons of nondairy milk, water, applesauce, banana, or oil, or try cooking the waffles for slightly less time.

If you wish to store & reheat leftovers

While nothing beats the flavor and texture of a freshly baked waffle, you'll find yourself in situations where you simply have more batter than you can consume. Also, you may wish to make a batch on the weekend and have an easy-to-prepare breakfast for a few mornings the following week. Fortunately, you can take a few steps to optimize the quality of your vegan waffle leftovers.

Once a batter is completely mixed so that the baking powder or baking soda has begun to react with the liquid, it should be baked within half an hour or so. If stored and baked later, a batter may produce relatively dense and unleavened waffles. Thus, the best method for using extra batter is to bake it right away, put any extra waffles in a tightly sealed container or bag, and place them in the refrigerator or freezer.

If you know in advance that you'll be storing and reheating some of the waffles, you may undercook them slightly so they're less likely to burn when you reheat them. If you like them extra crispy, just bake them the normal time. If you plan to reheat the waffles in a toaster with slots smaller than a whole waffle, cut them into quarters before freezing. Cutting a frozen waffle can be difficult.

If you plan to eat the waffles within a day, the refrigerator will work for some waffles, as will the freezer. For periods of 2 days to 1 week, use the freezer. Although waffles can be stored in the freezer for many weeks, the quality may vary greatly after a week or so. Lay the waffles completely flat in the freezer so they don't take on in a warped shape that won't fit the toaster or iron.

If the toaster makes waffles too crispy for your liking, you can reheat a waffle by putting it back into the preheated waffle iron for 1 to 2 minutes. A waffle iron seals in much of the waffle's remaining moisture while heating it, whereas a toaster may dry it out a bit more.

If you're cooking for a large group

When preparing for a party or other event, try each waffle you plan on baking at least once in advance, and keep track of how long they take to bake on your iron. It's hard to overemphasize the importance of this. At our 2006 waffle party I attempted felafel waffles with little prior experimentation. Witnesses of the wrenching tragedy can probably still recall the piles of crispy waffle crumbs or "vaffeldander" I picked out of the iron. Fortunately, a few guests devoured most of them, claiming they were still delicious. I had to use a clean backup iron, and spent half an hour restoring the other one to working condition the next morning.

The same caveat applies to the waffle iron itself. If you borrow a friend's iron, try it with your recipe in advance to see how long each waffle takes to bake, how much oil you need to spray on, and so on—don't try to determine all this the night of the party.

Yeast-Raised Waffle Tips

Yeast-raised waffles require some special treatment, but they're well worth it. First, because contact with metal can impede the growth of yeast, use a porcelain, glass, or plastic mixing bowl. Secondly, yeast-based batter requires time to rise—at least 1 1/2 hours for quick-rise active dry yeast, and at least 3 hours for regular active dry yeast. Without this time, your batter may not develop properly, and the waffles may be more likely to stick to the iron.

Thirdly, if the yeast is dissolved in water (or in one recipe, orange juice) that's too cool or too hot, it won't do its job. Use warm water between 105 and 115 degrees F. You can judge this by splashing a bit onto the sensitive skin of your inner wrist—it should feel warmer than lukewarm but not hot or painful.

You can use your oven to create a warm spot for the flour mixture to rise. Make sure the oven rack is low enough for the bowl to fit in the oven. Turn the oven on for 1 to 2 minutes at 200 degrees F. (It shouldn't actually reach 200 degrees, but just warm up slightly.) Turn off the oven, place the covered bowl on the rack, and close the oven door to keep in the warmth. If you wish to let the batter stand overnight, strengthening the yeast flavor, covering the bowl, and leaving it at room temperature will work fine. Wheat flour batters may come close to doubling, while gluten-free batters will expand less.

Additionally, yeast-raised waffle batters (except for gluten-free ones) require much more vigorous stirring than non-yeast batters. The yeast-raised portion may develop a "stringy" consistency that doesn't easily blend with the final ingredients added. Mixing with the handle end of a spoon or other thin item like chopsticks can make it easier to break up the long strands into smaller clumps. The batter does not need to be completely smooth, but you don't want too many clumps larger than the last segment of your pinky finger. As noted on page 32, chopsticks are great to keep on hand for several waffle-related purposes.

Finally, if you buy active dry yeast in 1/4-ounce packets (roughly 2 1/4 teaspoons), you'll often have some left over. If you clip or rubber band the packet shut, or seal it in a food storage bag, the yeast will keep in the refrigerator for up to 4 months.

Vegan Waffle Pantry Staples

While some vegan ingredients are very common, others may be less familiar. The following information is intended to make it easier to find the ingredients, to determine which waffles you're most likely to enjoy, to discern between different varieties of the same ingredient, and to judge which substitutions are more likely to work when necessary.

If you have a favorite non-vegan recipe that you'd like to convert into a great vegan dish or vegan waffle topping recipe, the below will also provide some substitution ideas for butter, eggs and milk taken from animals. If you can't find some of the items in your local grocery store, try to locate a local food co-op or a health foods store.

Alongside the items here, you'll want to keep a supply of the herbs and spices for your favorite waffles.

Flours, grains, & seeds utilized like flours

The recipes in this book use several types of flour. Because they have different properties, one can't always be substituted for another. Wheat flours generally have the highest gluten content, and the higher the gluten content, the greater the binding and elasticity of the waffle. Replacing wheat flour with a non-wheat ingredient may not work because the gluten content may no longer be high enough to provide proper binding or stick-togetherness—the waffles may split into two halves upon opening the iron. This is why recipes with non-wheat flours often incorporate additional binding ingredients.

While it's often safe to do the converse, replacing a non-wheat ingredient with a wheat ingredient, you may still need to adjust the liquid amount because some flours absorb more moisture than others. Additionally, different grains and seeds impart slightly different flavors.

Below are most of the flours, grains and seeds used in this book. Because ground flaxseed is utilized as a binder rather than a flour, it is discussed later under "Binders" (page 26).

All-purpose flour

Made from wheat, all-purpose flour has had some of the grain removed so it can be stored longer—unfortunately, some nutrition is also lost in this process. All-purpose flour is sometimes used alongside other flours like whole wheat to make the waffle lighter and fluffier. It can also be used alongside lower-gluten flours for additional binding. While the unbleached and bleached varieties will yield similar results, the unbleached flour involves less chemical processing.

Amaranth flour

Amaranth's colorful tufts produce thousands of tiny spherical seeds with a high protein content. The whole seed can be cooked in water and served warm as a breakfast cereal, or it can be ground into flour. Because the seed is so small, be careful not to confuse amaranth flour with non-ground amaranth seed.

Buckwheat flour

Despite the name, it is not related to wheat. If you're making waffles for someone with gluten or wheat sensitivities, be sure to get pure buckwheat flour that hasn't been cross-contaminated with wheat. Because some find the flavor of buckwheat flour overpowering, it is often used alongside a milder flour.

Cornmeal

Cornmeal is simply ground corn. Because it doesn't have sufficient binding properties on its own, it is used alongside flours and binders to create a crispier, slightly coarser texture, and a more toasted flavor. It should not be confused with corn flour, which is ground more finely and therefore behaves differently.

Hempseed

The Mucho Molassesey Vegan Power Waffles (page 97) use ground hempseed, also called hemp protein powder. Individuals engaging in above-average levels of athletic activity sometimes use it as a nutritional supplement. Thus, it is often carried in the nutritional supplements section of food and fitness stores. While large containers of ground hempseed can be relatively expensive, envelopes containing a few tablespoons are available. This product is not from the same plant that produces the currently illegal recreational substance.

Oats

This book references several forms of this common grain. Oats may be ground into flour. They may be chopped into small pieces with blades to form Irish or steel cut oats. They can be steamed and rolled into small, flat ovals to be sold as rolled oats. "Quick oats" are rolled oats that are sliced thinner and processed a bit more so they soften and cook faster. While quick oats can be substituted for standard rolled oats, they won't provide quite the same chewy texture that the less processed rolled oats will provide. Beyond this, the different forms of oats may not be used interchangeably without making other recipe adjustments.

Quinoa seed and flour

Pronounced "kee-NO-ah" or "KEEN-wah," the whole quinoa seed cooks similarly to grains, contains all the essential amino acids, and has a slightly nutty flavor. It is usually, but not always, processed to remove the saponin, a bitter substance coating the exterior. Place a few pieces on your tongue before cooking it or adding it to batter. If you detect a strong bitterness, do the following just before cooking: place it in a fine mesh strainer, rinse under cold water for 1 to 2 minutes, and drain. Because quinoa is relatively expensive in flour form, only one recipe in this book calls for it alongside the whole non-ground seed. (The flour form should never be rinsed!)

Rice flour

Rice flour is used in many of the gluten-free waffle recipes, and it is available in both white and brown rice versions. Brown rice flour has a higher nutritional content because it includes parts of the grain that are stripped away from white rice. You can generally replace brown rice flour with white rice flour for a slightly lighter and fluffier texture. However, unless a recipe specifies that either type will work, replacing white rice flour with brown rice flour could result in a slightly denser waffle that doesn't hold together as well.

Spelt flour

Related to wheat, spelt is not suitable for many people with wheat sensitivities, but some people who cannot digest wheat can digest spelt. It has less gluten, and creates waffles slightly less dense than those made with whole wheat flour.

Because spelt takes a little time to absorb moisture, recipes calling for it suggest letting the batter stand for a few additional minutes before baking.

Tapioca flour

Sometimes also called tapioca starch, this fine white powder is from the root of the cassava plant. It is often used alongside rice flour to aid thickness and chewiness in gluten-free recipes.

Teff grain and flour

If you've ever eaten in an Ethiopian restaurant, you've probably had a flat crepe-like bread called injera, which incorporates teff flour. It has a somewhat nutty flavor, is gluten-free, and adds a bit of crispiness to waffles. Non-ground teff grain is even smaller than amaranth, so be careful not to confuse teff flour with non-ground teff.

Whole wheat flour

This has more nutritional value than all-purpose wheat because it includes all parts of the grain. It has a high gluten content compared to the non-wheat flours listed here, so it binds well compared to other flours. The recipes here call for basic whole wheat flour. While flour labeled as "white whole wheat flour" will yield similar results, anything labeled as "whole wheat bread flour" or "whole wheat pastry flour" will yield a slightly different product. The latter two varieties have different levels of gluten, resulting in different levels of binding and chewiness.

Leaveners

In vegan waffle recipes, baking powder and baking soda provide plenty of leavening without eggs. Recipes using baking soda will also generally have an acidic item to react with it, such as vinegar, lemon juice, lime juice, molasses, brown sugar, soy yogurt, or applesauce.

As for yeast, you can use either the regular or quick rise active dry yeast that comes in 1/4-ounce packets, or in 4-ounce jars. Alongside making the dough rise, the slight fermentation adds additional flavor and texture to the waffle. For recipes here, the regular active dry yeast requires 3 hours minimum rising time compared to 1 1/2 hours minimum rising time for the quick rise variety.

Binders

In recipes that are based upon high-gluten flours such as wheat, and that contain few or no fillings, the flour itself usually provides plenty of binding or "stick togetherness." Baking powder, bananas, and applesauce can also add smaller levels of binding. For waffles that use low-gluten or gluten-free flours, or that incorporate a large volume of flavorful fillings, additional binding may be necessary. This is why many of the recipes incorporate ground flaxseed or xanthan gum.

You can purchase pre-ground flaxseed, sometimes labeled as flaxseed meal, or you can purchase it whole and grind it as finely as possible with a coffee grinder. Once ground, the shelf life of flax shortens considerably. If grinding yourself, refrigerate any unused portion in a sealed container, and use within a week. Otherwise, follow the storage directions on the label, as some pre-ground flaxseed is prepared in a way that extends the shelf life. Ground flaxseed also has other uses—some people put it on their breakfast cereal as a source of ALA (alpha-linolenic acid, of the omega-3 fatty acid family).

Xanthan gum powder serves both a thickening and binding function, and is used in several of the gluten-free recipes. It also adds a creamier texture to the ice cream recipes. Created by allowing bacteria to ferment sugars, it is sold as a powder. Because only 1 to 2 teaspoons (or less) is required for 4 waffles, an 8-ounce bag lasts a very long time.

If, after practice, you come to prefer the taste or texture of one binding ingredient better than the others, you may wish to experiment with substitutions. Things may not turn out perfectly at first because each binder behaves slightly differently, but you'll move even closer to Vegan Waffle Nirvana in the long run!

Liquids

The majority of recipes in this book were created using plain, unsweetened soymilk. Moderately sweetened soymilk will also work. If you have soy allergies or simply don't like soymilk, you can use nutmilks (e.g., almond milk or hazelnut milk), rice milk, hempseed milk, water, or coconut milk. However, because each liquid has a different thickness and ability to dissolve solids, you may need to adjust the amount slightly. Almond milk and rice milk, for example, are often slightly thinner than soymilk. Coconut milk contains a large amount of fat, so the amount of oil may need to be adjusted.

Sweeteners

These not only alter the flavor of the waffle, but also add caramelization and additional crispiness to the exterior.

Sugar

The recipes in this book were created with granulated unrefined or raw cane sugar. Sucanat, demerara, and turbinado sugars will yield similar results where only 1 or 2 tablespoons are required. For larger amounts, slight differences in darkness and flavor may occur. Refined white granulated sugar will also work, but many vegans prefer to avoid brands that filter their sugar through charred animal bone as part of the refining process. If you're baking for vegan friends and don't know where they stand on this, it's safest to ask or just use an unrefined sugar. Substituting a liquid sweetener such as agave or maple syrup may impact the properties of the waffles significantly. None of the recipes were tested with artificial granulated sugar substitutes.

Maple syrup

This refers to genuine maple syrup. However, it does not have to be the "grade A" variety. In fact, the recipes in this book were created with a less refined and often less expensive version sold as "grade B." When baked into items, there's no noticeable difference; and when used in toppings, the difference is slightly noticeable. Many people actually prefer the flavor of grade B syrup over grade A. Artificially-flavored syrups based upon corn syrup will make a close approximation, but may yield noticeable differences in some recipes.

Molasses

If you enjoy a pronounced molasses flavor, blackstrap molasses will work well. It is the darkest, strongest tasting, and most nutritionally condensed molasses, and was used in creating the recipes in this book. If you prefer a slightly sweeter and more subtle flavor, standard molasses will do the trick.

Sweeteners not used in this book

Some people prefer liquid alternatives to cane sugar, such as agave nectar or rice syrup. However, substituting liquid sweeteners may alter the baking properties, and may require other adjustments to the recipes. With topping recipes, this is less likely to be an issue.

Crushed or powdered stevia leaves are many times sweeter than sugar and offer an alternative sweetener for individuals with blood sugar issues. However, using stevia in lieu of a sugar-based sweetener will also change the baking properties of the waffles. Sugar caramelizes and adds crispiness, while stevia does not.

Oil & margarine

These ingredients provide fat to enhance moistness, increase flavor, improve the cooking process, and lessen sticking. Unlike their non-vegan counterparts such as butter, they have no cholesterol. Most waffle recipes call for canola oil, which has a relatively neutral flavor. Safflower oil or a vegetable oil mix will also work. Olive oil is not recommended unless a recipe calls for it, as it has a more pronounced flavor.

A number of toppings call for vegan margarine, mainly because it thickens a bit more. Because most margarine contains salt, oil and margarine cannot be substituted for one another without adjusting the salt content. Also note that "whipped" margarines may require slightly larger amounts because they may yield less when melted.

While applesauce can replace oil in some types of baking recipes, it is often difficult to prevent sticking with an entirely oil-free waffle. One exception is a waffle using a significant volume of coconut milk, which also has a high fat content. A few such recipes appear at WaffleParty.com.

As noted under "General Vegan Waffle Baking Tips" (page 17), it is important to oil both waffle iron grids prior to each waffle, even with a non-stick waffle iron and a batter containing oil. For this, a pressurized spray can of canola oil or another relatively neutrally-flavored cooking oil is a good option. Brushing on oil yields less consistent results, probably because it is more difficult to achieve full and even coverage.

While many brands of pressurized spray oil have eliminated the environmentally-unfriendly chloroflourocarbons (CFC's), I have tried the refillable oil spray bottles in an attempt to be even more environmentally friendly. Unfortunately, the ones I've tried didn't produce a fine enough mist to coat the iron evenly and sufficiently. However, your mileage may vary.

Vegan cream cheese & sour cream

While the hydrogenated versions of vegan cream cheese will result in slightly firmer baked goods, the recipes here were created with the healthier non-hydrogenated versions. Some stores keep these products alongside the dairy cream cheese and sour cream, while others group them with other non-dairy items.

Other not-so-common ingredients

Nutritional yeast

This deactivated yeast is grown on molasses, and it adds a rich, savory, cheese-like flavor in conjunction with other ingredients. It is sold in the form of thin, tan flakes, and sometimes as a powder, often in the bulk food section of co-ops and natural food stores. Some brands are fortified with vitamin B12.

Miso

Made by fermenting ingredients such as soybeans, chickpeas, or rice, this paste has a strong, savory, salty flavor. It is probably best known for its use in miso soup, and it plays an important role in some of the recipes with cheese-like overtones.

Carob powder

Derived from the pods of the carob tree, this rich-tasting ingredient is often suggested as a substitute for chocolate, although it has a noticeably different flavor. It does not contain stimulants as cocoa does, and is a bit sweeter. Like cocoa, it is often sold in powdered or chip form. The recipes here call for roasted carob powder, which has a different flavor than raw carob powder. However, this is a matter of personal preference, so you could substitute the raw version if you like it better.

Waffle Irons & Other Essential Equipment

While I cannot endorse particular brands or models of equipment here, I provide general suggestions for finding the tools that best suit your preferences.

Waffle irons

Without a waffle iron, you are limited to pancakes. A common question is, "How much should I spend on a waffle iron?" Great waffle irons can be found across a broad range of prices, depending upon the features and quality. Because models change frequently and quality is not always directly related to price, you'll need to do some homework. Here are some of the features to consider:

Wattage

As a rough rule of thumb, it's best to have something with at least 1,000 watts, or more if it's a large family-style waffle maker. A lower wattage usually means a lower temperature, especially when that energy is spread over a large baking

area. I've been pretty satisfied with 1,200 watts spread over an area of a 7-inch round Belgian waffle. Vegan waffles in general can take a bit longer to cook, and this is particularly the case with waffles with fillings. Sufficient wattage can help to compensate for this.

Manual temperature control

This is optional, but is useful for increasing the heat for waffles that are crispier on the outside and moister on the inside—or decreasing the heat to cook the outside and inside relatively evenly.

Built-in audio timer alarm or "done" light

This can be handy in lieu of an external cooking timer (see page 33). Note that some recipes may require more or less time, especially if they include many fillings. A few tries will yield a sense of how long to leave waffles in the iron following the signal. Some built-in timers may not work properly with waffles that don't fill the entire iron, e.g., if there's just enough batter remaining at the end to make half of a waffle.

Rotating or flipping grill

This feature allows you to "flip" the waffle as it begins to cook, helping the waffle to cook more evenly on both sides and making it slightly fluffier. It is not necessary, but it can make a noticeable difference, especially around the edges of the waffle. Just keep in mind that more moving parts sometimes means more opportunity for things to wear out or break, so be sure to consult some reviews of any flipping model you're considering.

Overflow catch tray

This can save a lot of time and hassle, as it will keep boiled-over batter and oil from flowing all over the counter. Dried batter can be a chore to scrape off. A cookie sheet can also serve as a catch tray.

Round versus square waffles, and depth of waffle holes

These are both a matter of personal preference. However, deeper holes hold syrups and toppings better.

If you're on a limited budget

While new waffle irons span a large range of quality and prices, used irons are also relatively easy to find. This may be because they are a popular gift item. Many people use their gifts only a few times, put them away in storage, and pull them back out several years—or even decades—later. If there are no thrift stores or upcoming moving sales nearby, a few neighbors or friends probably have an iron they'd be happy to lend—or perhaps even sell.

As the basic technology of waffle irons hasn't changed much over the years, most 20-year-old functional irons will bake a waffle in roughly the same manner as a brand new iron, minus the slight quality added by modern features such as a rotating grill. However, there are potential "wear and tear" items to look out for on used irons. These include faulty electrical cords and worn-off nonstick coating. Both of these wear out over time regardless, but the latter can be hastened if the owner used objects like metal forks to scrape out stuck-on waffles. Although it's important to spray the grids with oil prior to each waffle anyway, an intact nonstick surface still helps.

Ladle

Often used for soup and punch, this tool is also handy for getting the batter from the bowl into the iron with minimal spilling. It also provides a relatively easy way to measure the batter consistently.

Whisks, spoons, & spatulas

Wire whisks are handy for breaking up powdery clumps in the dry ingredient mixture, before adding the wet ingredients. This is particularly the case with cocoa and carob. Whisks are also great for breaking up clumps of peanut butter, miso, avocado, banana, softened margarine, and sometimes baking powder and baking soda.

For the final mixing, using a large spoon or a spatula (rubber or silicone) rather than a whisk can help to avoid overstirring. With the exception of yeast-raised waffles, removing all the lumps can create tough waffles. Spoons and spatulas are also helpful for folding in "filling" ingredients such as nuts near the end of stirring.

Chopsticks: Waffle rescuers & yeast dough stirrers

Chopsticks are useful for lifting waffles out of the iron, with a much lower risk of scratching the non-stick surface than metal forks pose. For very moist and cakelike waffles, sliding one chopstick under each side of a waffle (think of yourself and your chopsticks as a mini forklift) makes it easier to remove without breaking it into small pieces. As a stirring tool for yeast-raised recipes, chopsticks help to break up and incorporate the thicker and stringier yeast-raised portion into the ingredients added later. In the case of minor sticking, chopsticks fit into the crevices of the grid to scrape out stubborn pieces. (Just keep in mind that you can still harm the nonstick surface if scraping too hard.) A chopstick with a damp rag or paper towel wrapped around the tip is useful for cleaning the iron's grids occasionally.

Mashers

Several of the recipes call for thoroughly mashed banana, avocado, or potato. While a metal fork will do the trick, a potato masher will save time and effort in removing most of the lumps.

Graters & grinders

A handheld metal grater with relatively large holes, which may be sold as a cheese grater, may be used for carrots and fresh ginger. A food processor with a grating disc will also do the job. Graters with much smaller holes, sold as graters/zesters, microplane graters, or nutmeg graters, may be used for fresh ginger or nutmeg. Coffee bean grinders are useful for grinding flaxseed, and may be used to prepare freshly ground versions of certain spices such as cumin.

Timers

Even if an iron has a built-in "done" alarm, it may be more accurate for some types of waffles than others. This is where adjustable timers with displays are useful. A digital cooking timer, a wind-up spring powered timer, a watch timer, or a stove or microwave with a built-in timer will do the trick. (Just try not to get too much waffle batter on your watch!) Some waffle makers now have built-in timers with displays.

For waffle parties, I use 2 cooking timers that allow me to set a particular countdown time, and then stop and automatically restart at that same time with 2 simple button presses. This makes it easier to keep track of waffles in multiple irons. They also beep continuously until "stop" is pressed, unlike the 4 or 5 beeps of the irons' built-in timers that can be missed if I leave the kitchen temporarily. That can happen when cooking during a party.

Ice cream maker

This is not required for making waffles, but is needed for 3 of the sweet toppings in this book. As with waffle makers, many models exist across a broad price range. If you don't plan on making enough vegan ice cream or sorbet to justify the investment, simply purchase a pre-made frozen dessert to accompany your waffles whenever you crave a cold treat.

Batter bowls

It's important to have at least one large and one medium mixing bowl for making waffle batter. For yeast-raised waffles (see also "Yeast-Raised Waffle Tips" on page 21), non-metal materials such as porcelain, glass, or plastic are best. For preparing wet and dry portions ahead of time, bowls with sealable lids may be helpful.

Also available are "batter bowls" with a handle and a pouring spout. They often have measurement lines that may or may not be accurate enough for initial ingredient measurement, but it's still necessary to use visual estimation when pouring the batter into the iron. Make sure the bowl is dishwasher-safe if you don't plan to wash them by hand. (I learned this the hard way, after the dishwasher's heat created little cracks in mine.)

Flour sifter or fine wire mesh strainer

A number of recipes call for cocoa powder or carob powder, both of which can develop clumps. Vigorously stirring the dry ingredients with a wire whisk, adding the wet ingredients, and then breaking up any remaining clumps with a spoon or spatula is generally sufficient. Alternately, you can sift the cocoa or carob powder and flour together, through a flour sifter or fine wire mesh strainer, after measuring them. This will reduce clumping even more.

A sifter or fine wire mesh strainer can also be useful if you wish to sprinkle a thin and even layer of cocoa powder, carob powder, or powdered sugar across the surface of a waffle.

Neutral Waffles

These recipes rely upon a variety of grains, sweeteners, and yeast for much of their taste. While always flavorful, they are intended to be consumed with toppings, and are subtle enough to work with a very broad range of flavors—sweet or savory. This versatility makes them ideal for events where many toppings are present. The simpler recipes, like the Naked Vegan Waffles (page 37) are great if you're already extremely hungry or are otherwise short on preparation time. Those with a few more steps or ingredients, like the Yeast-Raised Waffles (page 42) or the Crispy Cornbuck Waffles (page 49), add specialness to a meal or celebration.

Naked Vegan Waffles

Makes 4 (7-inch) round Belgian waffles

A few visitors to WaffleParty.com requested a very simple, neutral waffle recipe to accompany the more adventurous recipes. This easy but still tasty treat has proven to be quite popular. For a minimalist approach, simply drizzle with melted margarine and warm maple syrup. Or, get crazy and spoon on some Black Bean-Mango Tango (page 121).

1 1/2 cups whole wheat flour
1 cup all-purpose flour
2 teaspoons baking powder
1 teaspoon baking soda
1 teaspoon salt
2 1/4 cups soymilk or other nondairy milk
1/4 cup canola oil
3 tablespoons brown sugar

Combine the whole wheat flour, all-purpose flour, baking powder, baking soda, and salt in a large bowl and stir with a whisk. Thoroughly mix the soymilk, oil, and brown sugar in a medium bowl. Pour into the flour mixture and stir just until blended.

Preheat the waffle iron for 3 to 5 minutes and spray both grids with oil. Pour or ladle the batter into the center of the iron, covering no more than two-thirds of the iron's surface for the first waffle. Adjust the amount as needed for subsequent waffles. Bake each waffle for 3 to 5 minutes, or until it can be removed easily.

Tropically Tanned Naked Waffles

Makes 4 (7-inch) round Belgian waffles

These exude a bit more crispiness and sweetness than the Naked Vegan Waffles (page 37), and the molasses overtones add a hint of complexity. For a true tropical flavor, pour on some Very Coconutty Syrup (page 106).

1 1/2 cups whole wheat flour
1 cup all-purpose flour
2 teaspoons baking powder
1 teaspoon baking soda
1 1/4 teaspoons salt
2 1/4 cups soymilk or other nondairy milk
1/4 cup plus 2 tablespoons canola oil
1/4 cup brown sugar
2 tablespoons molasses (blackstrap or other variety)

Combine the whole wheat flour, all-purpose flour, baking powder, baking soda, and salt in a large bowl and stir with a whisk. Thoroughly mix the soymilk, oil, brown sugar, and molasses in a medium bowl. Pour into the flour mixture and stir just until blended.

Preheat the waffle iron for 3 to 5 minutes and spray both grids with oil. Pour or ladle the batter into the center of the iron, covering no more than two-thirds of the iron's surface for the first waffle. Adjust the amount as needed for subsequent waffles. Bake each waffle for 3 to 5 minutes, or until it can be removed easily.

Mapley Waffles (GF)

Makes 4 (7-inch) round Belgian waffles

These are cousins of the Naked Vegan Waffles (page 37), plus baked-in maple flavor, minus the wheat. To increase the sweetness and texture, sprinkle with brown sugar and crushed walnuts.

> 1 3/4 cups brown rice flour
> 1/2 cup tapioca flour
> 2 teaspoons baking powder
> 1 teaspoon baking soda
> 1 teaspoon salt
> 1 1/2 teaspoons xanthan gum powder
> 2 cups soymilk or other nondairy milk
> 1/2 cup canola oil
> 1/2 cup maple syrup
> 1 1/2 teaspoons vanilla extract

Combine the brown rice flour, tapioca flour, baking powder, baking soda, salt, and xanthan gum powder in a large bowl and stir with a whisk. Thoroughly mix the soymilk, oil, maple syrup, and vanilla extract in a medium bowl. Pour into the flour mixture and stir just until blended. Let stand for 4 to 5 minutes.

Preheat the waffle iron for 3 to 5 minutes while the batter is standing. Spray both grids of the waffle iron with oil. Pour or ladle the batter into the center of the iron, covering no more than two-thirds of the iron's surface for the first waffle. Adjust the amount as needed for subsequent waffles. Bake each waffle for 3 to 5 minutes, or until it can be removed easily.

Sinfully Cinnamon Mapley Waffles: Add 1 1/2 teaspoons ground cinnamon to the flour mixture.

Nice Rice-Teff Waffles (GF)

Makes 4 (7-inch) round Belgian waffles

These are just a little crispier and slightly sweeter than the Mapley Waffles (page 39). The teff flour takes it to a wholenutha level. For a special treat or a decadent breakfast, sandwich a few scoops of Mango-Vanilla Ice Cream (page 113) between 2 waffle quarters.

1 1/4 cups brown rice flour
1/2 cup tapioca flour
1/2 cup teff flour
2 teaspoons baking powder
1 teaspoon baking soda
1 1/4 teaspoons salt
1 teaspoon xanthan gum powder
1 3/4 cups plus 2 tablespoons soymilk or other nondairy milk
1/4 cup plus 2 tablespoons brown sugar
1/4 cup plus 2 tablespoons canola oil
1/4 cup maple syrup
1 1/2 teaspoons vanilla extract

Combine the brown rice flour, tapioca flour, teff flour, baking powder, baking soda, salt, and xanthan gum powder in a large bowl and stir with a whisk. Thoroughly mix the soymilk, brown sugar, oil, maple syrup, and vanilla extract in a medium bowl. Pour into the flour mixture and stir just until blended. Let stand for 4 to 5 minutes.

Preheat the waffle iron for 3 to 5 minutes while the batter is standing. Spray both grids of the waffle iron with oil. Pour or ladle the batter into the center of the iron, covering no more than two-thirds of the iron's surface for the first waffle. Adjust the amount as needed for subsequent waffles. Bake each waffle for 3 to 5 minutes, or until it can be removed easily.

Textured Rice Waffles (GF)

Makes 4 (7-inch) round Belgian waffles

These siblings of the Nice Rice-Teff Waffles (page 40) replace the teff flour with the increased texture of whole teff grain, and utilize ground flaxseed in lieu of xanthan gum. Serve up with a topping of sliced banana and Maple Syrup Supreme (page 104), or heat some peanut butter and pour it on.

1 1/2 cups brown rice flour
1/2 cup tapioca flour
1/4 cup whole teff grain
2 teaspoons baking powder
1 teaspoon baking soda
1 1/4 teaspoons salt
2 cups soymilk or other nondairy milk
1/4 cup plus 2 tablespoons brown sugar
1/4 cup plus 2 tablespoons canola oil
1/4 cup ground flaxseed
1/4 cup maple syrup
1 1/2 teaspoons vanilla extract

Combine the brown rice flour, tapioca flour, teff grain, baking powder, baking soda, and salt in a large bowl and stir with a whisk. Thoroughly mix the soymilk, brown sugar, oil, flaxseed, maple syrup, and vanilla extract in a medium bowl. Pour into the flour mixture and stir just until blended. Let stand for 4 to 5 minutes.

Preheat the waffle iron for 3 to 5 minutes while the batter is standing. Spray both grids of the waffle iron with oil. Pour or ladle the batter into the center of the iron, covering no more than two-thirds of the iron's surface for the first waffle. Adjust the amount as needed for subsequent waffles. Bake each waffle for 3 to 5 minutes, or until it can be removed easily.

Yeast-Raised Waffles

Makes 3 to 4 (7-inch) round Belgian waffles

These have a flavor reminiscent of sourdough bread, and a thin, crispy crust that's missing from most waffles. Because the dough needs time to rise, begin at least 3 hours in advance of baking the waffles or 1 1/2 hours in advance if you are using quick-rise yeast. Spoon on some fruit preserves and melted margarine.

> 1 1/4 teaspoons active dry yeast
> 1 1/2 cups warm water (see "Yeast-Raised Waffle Tips," page 21)
> 1 1/2 cups whole wheat flour
> 1/2 cup all-purpose flour
> 1 1/2 teaspoons salt
> 1/2 cup plus 2 tablespoons soymilk or other nondairy milk
> 1/4 cup canola oil
> 3 tablespoons brown sugar
> 1/2 teaspoon baking powder
> 1/2 teaspoon baking soda

Dissolve the yeast in the water in a large non-metal bowl. Let stand for 5 minutes. Stir in the whole wheat flour, all-purpose flour, and salt until well blended. Cover the bowl and place it in a warm location until the flour mixture has almost doubled (see "Yeast-Raised Waffle Tips," page 21).

After the flour mixture has risen, combine the soymilk, oil, brown sugar, baking powder, and baking soda in a small bowl. Mix thoroughly, breaking up any clumps of baking powder or baking soda. Pour into the raised flour mixture and stir until well blended. Let stand for 15 minutes.

Preheat the waffle iron for 3 to 5 minutes while the batter is standing. Spray both grids of the waffle iron with oil. Pour or ladle the batter into the center of the iron, covering no more than two-thirds of the iron's surface for the first waffle. Adjust the amount as needed for subsequent waffles. Bake each waffle for 3 to 5 minutes, or until it can be removed easily.

Slightly Teffy Yeast-Raised Waffles: Reduce the whole wheat flour to 1 1/4 cup plus 2 tablespoons. After the flour mixture has risen, while adding the soymilk and remaining ingredients, add 1/4 cup of whole teff grain.

Sweet Yeast-Raised Waffles

Makes 4 (7-inch) round Belgian waffles

Compared to the Yeast-Raised Waffles (page 42), these are a little denser on the inside and slightly crispier on the outside. Because the dough needs time to rise, begin at least 3 hours in advance of baking the waffles or 1 1/2 hours in advance if you are using quick-rise yeast. Enjoy with Carob Halvah Spread (page 111).

1 1/4 teaspoons active dry yeast
1 1/2 cups warm water (see "Yeast-Raised Waffle Tips," page 21)
1 cup all-purpose flour
1 cup whole wheat flour
1 1/2 teaspoons salt
1/4 cup brown sugar
1/4 cup canola oil
1/4 cup maple syrup
1/4 cup soymilk or other nondairy milk
1 teaspoon vanilla extract
3/4 teaspoon baking powder
1/2 teaspoon baking soda

Dissolve the yeast in the water in a large non-metal bowl. Let stand for 5 minutes. Stir in the whole wheat flour, all-purpose flour, and salt until well blended. Cover the bowl and place it in a warm location until the flour mixture has almost doubled (see "Yeast-Raised Waffle Tips," page 21).

After the flour mixture has risen, combine the brown sugar, oil, maple syrup, soymilk, vanilla extract, baking powder, and baking soda in a small bowl. Mix thoroughly, breaking up any clumps of baking powder or baking soda. Pour into the raised flour mixture and stir until well blended. Let stand for 15 minutes.

Preheat the waffle iron for 3 to 5 minutes while the batter is standing. Spray both grids of the waffle iron with oil. Pour or ladle the batter into the center of the iron, covering no more than two-thirds of the iron's surface for the first waffle. Adjust the amount as needed for subsequent waffles. Bake each waffle for 3 to 5 minutes, or until it can be removed easily.

Pass the Buckwheat-Oat Waffles

Makes 3 to 4 (7-inch) round Belgian waffles

These wholesome-tasting treats allow the buckwheat's pronounced flavor to shine through. Top with a hearty helping of applesauce and maple syrup, or for an even heartier treat, spoon on some Savory Cashew-Mushroom Sauce (page 117).

    1 cup buckwheat flour
    1/2 cup all-purpose flour
    1/2 cup rolled oats
    2 teaspoons baking powder
    1/2 teaspoon baking soda
    3/4 teaspoon salt
    1 3/4 cups soymilk or other nondairy milk
    1/3 cup smooth applesauce
    2 tablespoons brown sugar
    2 tablespoons canola oil
    2 tablespoons ground flaxseed
    1 teaspoon vanilla extract

Combine the buckwheat flour, all-purpose flour, oats, baking powder, baking soda, and salt in a large bowl and stir with a whisk. Thoroughly mix the soymilk, applesauce, brown sugar, oil, ground flaxseed, and vanilla extract in a medium bowl. Pour into the flour mixture and stir just until blended. Let stand for 5 minutes.

Preheat the waffle iron for 3 to 5 minutes while the batter is standing. Spray both grids of the waffle iron with oil. Pour or ladle the batter into the center of the iron, covering no more than two-thirds of the iron's surface for the first waffle. Adjust the amount as needed for subsequent waffles. Bake each waffle for 3 to 5 minutes, or until it can be removed easily.

Heartfelt Banana-Spelt Waffles

Makes 3 to 4 (7-inch) round Belgian waffles

These feature the unique lightness and fluffiness of spelt, joined with natural banana-laden sweetness. When you bake them for someone, they'll know that you care. For an extra burst of banananess, pour some Banana-Maple-Nut Syrup (page 102) all over them.

> 2 1/4 cups spelt flour
> 2 teaspoons baking powder
> 1/2 teaspoon salt
> 1 ripe banana, mashed until smooth
> 2 cups soymilk or other nondairy milk
> 1/4 cup canola oil
> 2 tablespoons brown sugar
> 2 tablespoons ground flaxseed
> 1 teaspoon vanilla extract

Combine the flour, baking powder, and salt in a large bowl and stir with a whisk. Mash the banana in a medium bowl, and thoroughly mix with the soymilk, oil, brown sugar, ground flaxseed, and vanilla extract. Pour into the flour mixture and stir just until blended. Let stand for 2 to 3 minutes. Stir 4 or 5 strokes, and then let stand 5 more minutes.

Preheat the waffle iron for 3 to 5 minutes while the batter is standing. Spray both grids of the waffle iron with oil. Pour or ladle the batter into the center of the iron, covering no more than two-thirds of the iron's surface for the first waffle. Adjust the amount as needed for subsequent waffles. Bake each waffle for 4 to 6 minutes, or until it can be removed easily.

Yeast-Raised Buckwheat Waffles (GF)

Makes 4 (7-inch) round Belgian waffles

Combining pronounced buckwheat flavor with yeast overtones, these possess a slight crispiness while being great syrup sponges. Because the dough needs time to rise, begin at least 3 hours in advance of baking the waffles or 1 1/2 hours in advance if you are using quick-rise yeast. Top with raspberries, blueberries, and a generous drizzling of Maple Syrup Supreme (page 104).

> 1 1/4 teaspoons active dry yeast
> 1 3/4 cups warm water (see "Yeast-Raised Waffle Tips," page 21)
> 1 cup buckwheat flour
> 1 cup brown or white rice flour
> 1 teaspoon salt
> 1/3 cup soymilk or other nondairy milk
> 3 tablespoons canola oil
> 2 tablespoons molasses (blackstrap or other variety)
> 1 teaspoon baking soda

Dissolve the yeast in the warm water in a large non-metal bowl. Let stand for 5 minutes. Stir in the buckwheat flour, rice flour, and salt until well blended. Cover the bowl and place it in a warm location so the flour mixture can expand to around 1 1/2 times its original volume. (See "Yeast-Raised Waffle Tips," page 21).

After the flour mixture has risen, combine the soymilk, oil, molasses, and baking soda in a small bowl. Mix thoroughly, breaking up any clumps of baking soda. Pour into the raised flour mixture and stir until well blended. Let stand for 15 minutes.

Preheat the waffle iron for 3 to 5 minutes while the batter is standing. Spray both grids of the waffle iron with oil. Pour or ladle the batter into the center of the iron, covering no more than two-thirds of the iron's surface for the first waffle. Adjust the amount as needed for subsequent waffles. Bake each waffle for 3 to 5 minutes, or until it can be removed easily.

Buckwheat-Molasses Waffles (GF)

Makes 4 (7-inch) round Belgian waffles

Alongside having no yeast, these are slightly sweeter than the Yeast-Raised Buckwheat Waffles (page 46), but still have a pronounced buckwheat flavor. Round out the picture with fresh blackberries and a dollop of vegan vanilla ice cream.

    1 cup buckwheat flour
    1 cup white rice flour
    1/2 cup tapioca flour
    2 teaspoons baking powder
    1 teaspoon baking soda
    1 teaspoon salt
    2 teaspoons xanthan gum powder
    2 1/2 cups soymilk or other nondairy milk
    1/4 cup canola oil
    2 tablespoons sugar
    2 tablespoons molasses (blackstrap or other variety)

Combine the buckwheat flour, white rice flour, tapioca flour, baking powder, baking soda, salt, and xanthan gum powder in a large bowl and stir with a whisk. Thoroughly mix the soymilk, oil, sugar, and molasses in a medium bowl. Pour into the flour mixture and stir just until blended. Let stand for 3 to 5 minutes.

Preheat the waffle iron for 3 to 5 minutes while the batter is standing. Spray both grids of the waffle iron with oil. Pour or ladle the batter into the center of the iron, covering no more than two-thirds of the iron's surface for the first waffle. Adjust the amount as needed for subsequent waffles. Bake each waffle for 4 to 5 minutes, or until it can be removed easily.

Crunchy Steel City Waffles (GF)

Makes 4 (7-inch) round Belgian waffles

These champions feature bits of chewy steel-cut oats and a hint of molasses to satisfy your tough side. Bump them up a notch with the Creamy Spiced Apple Pie Sauce (page 110).

> 1 3/4 cups brown rice flour
> 1/2 cup tapioca flour
> 1/4 cup uncooked steel-cut oats
> 2 teaspoons baking powder
> 1 teaspoon baking soda
> 3/4 teaspoon salt
> 1 teaspoon xanthan gum powder
> 1 1/2 cups soymilk or other nondairy milk
> 1/2 cup smooth applesauce
> 1/4 cup canola oil
> 1/4 cup maple syrup
> 2 tablespoons molasses (blackstrap or other variety)
> 1 teaspoon vanilla extract

Combine the brown rice flour, tapioca flour, oats, baking powder, baking soda, salt, and xanthan gum powder in a large bowl and stir with a whisk. Thoroughly mix the soymilk, applesauce, oil, maple syrup, molasses, and vanilla extract in a medium bowl. Pour into the flour mixture and stir just until blended. Let stand for 3 to 5 minutes.

Preheat the waffle iron for 3 to 5 minutes while the batter is standing. Spray both grids of the waffle iron with oil. Pour or ladle the batter into the center of the iron, covering no more than two-thirds of the iron's surface for the first waffle. Adjust the amount as needed for subsequent waffles. Bake each waffle for 3 to 5 minutes, or until it can be removed easily.

Crispy Cornbuck Waffles (GF)

Makes 4 (7-inch) round Belgian waffles

A waffle with a name that sounds like a cartoon hero, Crispy Cornbuck is a powerful culinary force. He just might save your day. Partner with the savory heartiness of Southwestern Beans and Greens (page 122), or the country-style sweetness of Maple Syrup Supreme (page 104).

> 2/3 cup brown rice flour
> 2/3 cup buckwheat flour
> 2/3 cup cornmeal
> 1/2 cup tapioca flour
> 2 teaspoons baking powder
> 1 teaspoon baking soda
> 1 teaspoon salt
> 2 cups soymilk or other nondairy milk
> 1/4 cup canola oil
> 1/4 cup ground flaxseed
> 1/4 cup maple syrup
> 1/4 cup water
> 2 tablespoons molasses (blackstrap or other variety)

Combine the brown rice flour, buckwheat flour, cornmeal, tapioca flour, baking powder, baking soda, and salt in a large bowl and stir with a whisk. Thoroughly mix the soymilk, oil, ground flaxseed, maple syrup, water, and molasses in a medium bowl. Pour into the flour mixture and stir just until blended. Let stand for 3 to 5 minutes.

Preheat the waffle iron for 3 to 5 minutes while the batter is standing. Spray both grids of the waffle iron with oil. Pour or ladle the batter into the center of the iron, covering no more than two-thirds of the iron's surface for the first waffle. Adjust the amount as needed for subsequent waffles. Bake each waffle for 3 to 5 minutes, or until it can be removed easily.

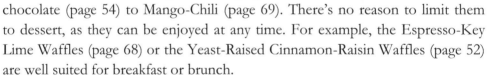

Flavory-Sweet Waffles

While the Neutral Waffles section contains some relatively sweet recipes, the waffles in this section blend sweetness with rich flavor combinations. These range from ginger-lemon-chocolate (page 54) to Mango-Chili (page 69). There's no reason to limit them to dessert, as they can be enjoyed at any time. For example, the Espresso-Key Lime Waffles (page 68) or the Yeast-Raised Cinnamon-Raisin Waffles (page 52) are well suited for breakfast or brunch.

Original Cinnamon-Raisin Waffles

Makes 5 (7-inch) round Belgian waffles

This classic flavor combination is great for any occasion, and this version can be prepared on shorter notice than the Yeast-Raised Cinnamon-Raisin Waffles (page 52). For a level of sweetness approximating a cinnamon roll, drizzle generously with Cinnamon Cream Cheese (page 108). Finely chopped walnuts add a flavorful topping twist.

> 1 1/4 cups all-purpose flour
> 1 cup whole wheat flour
> 1/2 cup rolled oats
> 2 teaspoons baking powder
> 1 teaspoon baking soda
> 1 1/2 teaspoons salt
> 1 tablespoon ground cinnamon
> 2 cups soymilk or other nondairy milk
> 1/2 cup brown sugar
> 1/2 cup canola oil
> 1/4 cup maple syrup
> 1 1/2 teaspoons vanilla extract
> 1/2 cup raisins

Combine the all-purpose flour, whole wheat flour, oats, baking powder, baking soda, salt, and cinnamon in a large bowl and stir with a whisk. Thoroughly mix the soymilk, brown sugar, oil, maple syrup, and vanilla extract in a medium bowl. Pour into the flour mixture and stir just until blended. Fold in the raisins.

Preheat the waffle iron for 3 to 5 minutes and spray both grids with oil. Pour or ladle the batter into the center of the iron, covering no more than two-thirds of the iron's surface for the first waffle. Adjust the amount as needed for subsequent waffles. Bake each waffle for 3 to 4 minutes, or until it can be removed easily.

Yeast-Raised Cinnamon-Raisin Waffles

Makes 5 (7-inch) round Belgian waffles

These deliver the same delicious flavor combination as the Original Cinnamon-Raisin Waffles (page 51), with a chewier, bread-like texture. They're a great brunch alternative to French toast, and they make a great dessert when covered with Cinnamon Cream Cheese (page 108). Because the dough needs time to rise, begin at least 3 hours in advance of baking the waffles or 1 1/2 hours in advance if you are using quick-rise yeast.

> 1 1/4 teaspoons active dry yeast
> 1 1/2 cups warm water (see "Yeast-Raised Waffle Tips," page 21)
> 1 cup all-purpose flour
> 3/4 cup whole wheat flour
> 3/4 cup rolled oats
> 1/4 cup maple syrup
> 1 1/2 teaspoons salt
> 1/2 cup soymilk or other nondairy milk
> 1/2 cup brown sugar
> 1/4 cup plus 2 tablespoons canola oil
> 2 tablespoons cider vinegar
> 1 tablespoon ground cinnamon
> 1 1/2 teaspoons vanilla extract
> 3/4 teaspoon baking soda
> 1/2 teaspoon baking powder
> 1/2 cup raisins

Dissolve the yeast in the water in a large non-metal bowl. Let stand for 5 minutes. Stir in the all-purpose flour, whole wheat flour, oats, syrup, and salt until well blended. Cover the bowl and place it in a warm location until the flour mixture has almost doubled (see "Yeast-Raised Waffle Tips," page 21).

After the flour mixture has risen, combine the soymilk, brown sugar, oil, vinegar, cinnamon, vanilla extract, baking soda, and baking powder in a small bowl. Mix thoroughly, breaking up any clumps of baking soda or baking powder. Pour into the raised flour mixture and stir until well blended. Fold in the raisins and let stand for 15 minutes.

Preheat the waffle iron for 3 to 5 minutes while the batter is standing. Spray both grids of the waffle iron with oil. Pour or ladle the batter into the center of the iron, covering no more than two-thirds of the iron's surface for the first waffle. Adjust the amount as needed for subsequent waffles. Bake each waffle for 3 to 4 minutes, or until it can be removed easily.

Generously Ginger-Lemon-Chocolate Waffles

Makes 4 to 5 (7-inch) round Belgian waffles

If you're a gingerchocolafanatic, these will hit the spot. They incorporate both fresh and candied ginger for enhanced warmth. Top with vegan ice cream and Dark Chocolate Syrup (page 101), Crazeee Carob Syrup (page 102), or Lemon-Ginger Drizzle (page 106).

1/4 cup semisweet chocolate or carob chips, finely chopped
1/4 cup candied ginger, finely chopped
1 tablespoon plus 1 teaspoon fresh grated ginger root
1 1/2 cups all-purpose flour
1 cup whole wheat flour
2 teaspoons baking powder
1 teaspoon baking soda
1 teaspoon salt
1 1/2 cups soymilk or other nondairy milk
1 cup sugar
1/4 cup plus 2 tablespoons canola oil
1/4 cup lemon juice
1 teaspoon vanilla extract

Chop the chocolate chips and candied ginger, grate the ginger root, and set aside. Combine the all-purpose flour, whole wheat flour, baking powder, baking soda, and salt in a large bowl and stir with a whisk. Thoroughly mix the fresh grated ginger root, soymilk, sugar, oil, lemon juice, and vanilla extract in a medium bowl. Pour into the flour mixture and stir just until blended. Fold in the chocolate chips and candied ginger.

Preheat the waffle iron for 3 to 5 minutes and spray both grids with oil. Pour or ladle the batter into the center of the iron, covering no more than two-thirds of the iron's surface for the first waffle. Adjust the amount as needed for subsequent waffles. Bake each waffle for 3 to 4 minutes, or until it can be removed easily.

Banana-Blueberry-Teff Waffles (GF)

Makes 4 (7-inch) round Belgian waffles

These deliver whole-grain flavor, slight tartness, and just a little crunch. Liven them up even more with a drizzle of maple syrup, strawberry jam, or Banana-Maple-Nut Syrup (page 102).

> 1 cup frozen blueberries, defrosted to room temperature
> 1 cup brown rice flour
> 3/4 cup teff flour
> 2 teaspoons baking powder
> 1 teaspoon baking soda
> 3/4 teaspoon salt
> 1/2 teaspoon xanthan gum powder
> 1 teaspoon ground cinnamon
> 2 ripe bananas, mashed until smooth
> 1 1/2 cups soymilk or other nondairy milk
> 1/2 cup plain soy yogurt
> 3 tablespoons canola oil
> 2 tablespoons brown sugar
> 1 teaspoon vanilla extract

Defrost and drain the blueberries, and set aside. (If the liquid from the blueberries is flavorful, you can save it to add to maple syrup for a topping.) Combine the rice flour, teff flour, baking powder, baking soda, salt, xanthan gum powder, and cinnamon in a large bowl and stir with a whisk. Mash the bananas in a medium bowl, and thoroughly mix with the soymilk, soy yogurt, oil, brown sugar, and vanilla extract. Pour into the flour mixture and stir just until blended. Fold in the defrosted blueberries. Let stand for 3 to 4 minutes.

Preheat the waffle iron for 3 to 5 minutes while the batter is standing. Spray both grids of the waffle iron with oil. Pour or ladle the batter into the center of the iron, covering no more than two-thirds of the iron's surface for the first waffle. Adjust the amount as needed for subsequent waffles. Bake each waffle for 4 to 5 minutes, or until it can be removed easily.

Crispy Maple-Cashew Waffles (GF)

Makes 4 (7-inch) round Belgian waffles

Relatively basic with just a little flair, these have a high COFI (Crispy Outside and Fluffy Inside) factor. Embellish with additional cashews, Dark Chocolate Syrup (page 101), or Maple Syrup Supreme (page 104).

3/4 cup raw cashews, finely chopped
1 1/4 cup brown rice flour
1/2 cup tapioca flour
1/2 cup teff flour
2 teaspoons baking powder
1 teaspoon baking soda
1 1/4 teaspoons salt
1 teaspoon xanthan gum powder
1/2 teaspoon ground cinnamon (optional)
1 3/4 cups soymilk or other nondairy milk
3/4 cup maple syrup
1/4 cup plus 2 tablespoons canola oil
1 teaspoon vanilla extract

Chop the cashews and set aside. Combine the rice flour, tapioca flour, teff flour, baking powder, baking soda, salt, xanthan gum powder, and cinnamon in a large bowl and stir with a whisk. Thoroughly mix the soymilk, maple syrup, oil, and vanilla extract in a medium bowl. Pour into the flour mixture and stir just until blended. Fold in the cashews. Let stand for 3 to 4 minutes.

Preheat the waffle iron for 3 to 5 minutes while the batter is standing. Spray both grids of the waffle iron with oil. Pour or ladle the batter into the center of the iron, covering no more than two-thirds of the iron's surface for the first waffle. Adjust the amount as needed for subsequent waffles. Bake each waffle for 3 to 4 minutes, or until it can be removed easily.

Dark Chocolate Cake Waffles

Makes 5 (7-inch) round Belgian waffles

Are you craving cake but don't feel like waiting for it to bake in the oven? Enjoy these delectable desserts with Cocoa or Carob Agave Nectar (page 103), Coco Kah-banana Syrup (page 105), or Creamy Maple-Chai Dream Sauce (page 109). Or, top with fresh strawberries or raspberries for a bit of tartness and color.

1 1/2 cups all-purpose flour
1/2 cup whole wheat flour
1/2 cup cocoa powder
1 1/2 teaspoons baking powder
1 teaspoon baking soda
1 teaspoon salt
2 1/3 cups soymilk or other nondairy milk
3/4 cup canola oil
1/2 cup plus 2 tablespoons brown sugar
2 teaspoons vanilla extract

Combine the all-purpose flour, whole wheat flour, cocoa powder, baking powder, baking soda, and salt in a large bowl and stir with a whisk. Break up any clumps of cocoa. Thoroughly mix the soymilk, oil, brown sugar, and vanilla extract in a medium bowl. Pour into the flour mixture and stir just until blended. If necessary, use a spoon or spatula to break up any new cocoa clumps and push the cocoa down into the batter.

Preheat the waffle iron for 3 to 5 minutes and spray both grids with oil. Pour or ladle the batter into the center of the iron, covering no more than two-thirds of the iron's surface for the first waffle. Adjust the amount as needed for subsequent waffles. Bake each waffle for 2 to 4 minutes, or until it is still moist but can be removed easily.

Hot Chocolate-Molasses Waffles

Makes 5 to 6 (7-inch) round Belgian waffles

Dark, sweet chocolate and spice warm up the taste buds. These moist, cakelike treats can follow dinner, or you can serve them to that special someone for a breakfast or brunch in bed. For added flare, garnish with chocolate chips and a dusting of cinnamon.

> 1 1/2 cups all-purpose flour
> 1/2 cup whole wheat flour
> 1/2 cup cocoa powder
> 1 1/2 teaspoons baking powder
> 1 teaspoon baking soda
> 1 teaspoon salt
> 1 1/2 teaspoons chili powder
> 1/8 teaspoon ground cayenne
> 2 1/4 cups soymilk or other nondairy milk
> 3/4 cup canola oil
> 1/2 cup sugar
> 1/4 cup molasses (blackstrap or other variety)
> 1 teaspoon vanilla extract

Combine the all-purpose flour, whole wheat flour, cocoa powder, baking powder, baking soda, salt, chili powder, and cayenne in a large bowl and stir with a whisk. Break up any clumps of cocoa. Thoroughly mix the soymilk, oil, sugar, molasses, and vanilla extract in a small bowl. Pour into the flour mixture and stir just until blended. If necessary, use a spoon or spatula to break up any new cocoa clumps and push the cocoa down into the batter.

Preheat the waffle iron for 3 to 5 minutes and spray both grids with oil. Pour or ladle the batter into the center of the iron, covering no more than two-thirds of the iron's surface for the first waffle. Adjust the amount as needed for subsequent waffles. Bake each waffle for 3 to 4 minutes, or until it is still moist but can be removed easily.

Coconut-Date Waffles (GF)

Makes 4 (7-inch) round Belgian waffles

These are chewy and filling, with a slightly macaroonish texture added by the coconut, and the unique sweetness of dates. Enjoy solo, or top with Dark Chocolate Syrup (page 101) or Crazeee Carob Syrup (page 102).

    3/4 cup dates, pitted and finely chopped
    1 1/2 cups brown or white rice flour
    1/2 cup tapioca flour
    2 teaspoons baking powder
    1 teaspoon baking soda
    3/4 teaspoon salt
    2 teaspoons xanthan gum powder
    1 cup finely shredded unsweetened coconut (macaroon style)
    1 1/2 cups coconut milk (not the "light" variety)
    1 1/4 cups water
    1/4 cup brown sugar
    1 teaspoon vanilla extract

Chop the dates and set aside. Combine the rice flour, tapioca flour, baking powder, baking soda, salt, xanthan gum powder, and coconut in a large bowl and stir with a whisk. Thoroughly mix the coconut milk, water, brown sugar, and vanilla extract in a medium bowl. Pour into the flour mixture and stir just until blended. Fold in the dates. Let stand for 3 to 4 minutes.

Preheat the waffle iron for 3 to 5 minutes while the batter is standing. Spray both grids of the waffle iron with oil. Pour or ladle the batter into the center of the iron, covering no more than two-thirds of the iron's surface for the first waffle. Adjust the amount as needed for subsequent waffles. Bake each waffle for 4 to 6 minutes, or until it can be removed easily.

PBMax (Peanut Butter to the Max) Waffles

Makes 4 (7-inch) round Belgian waffles

What is the maximum amount of peanut butter a batter can contain and still become a waffle? These waffles appear to come close. Garnish with Cocoa or Carob Agave Nectar (page 103), Dark Chocolate Syrup (page 101), jelly or jam, or sliced bananas.

> 1/2 cup all-purpose flour
> 1/2 cup whole wheat flour
> 1/4 cup rolled oats
> 1 teaspoon baking powder
> 3/4 teaspoon baking soda
> 3/4 teaspoon salt
> 1/2 teaspoon xanthan gum powder
> 1 1/4 cups soymilk or other nondairy milk
> 3/4 cup smooth peanut butter, salted (see note)
> 1/2 cup smooth applesauce
> 1/4 cup brown sugar
> 3 tablespoons canola oil
> 1 teaspoon vanilla extract

Combine the all-purpose flour, whole wheat flour, oats, baking powder, baking soda, salt, and xanthan gum powder in a large bowl and stir with a whisk. Thoroughly mix the soymilk, peanut butter, applesauce, brown sugar, oil, and vanilla extract in a small bowl. Pour into the flour mixture and stir just until blended. Let stand for 3 to 4 minutes.

Preheat the waffle iron for 3 to 5 minutes while the batter is standing. Spray both grids of the waffle iron with oil. Pour or ladle the batter into the center of the iron, covering no more than two-thirds of the iron's surface for the first waffle. Adjust the amount as needed for subsequent waffles. Bake each waffle for 3 to 4 minutes, or until it can be removed easily.

Note: If you're using peanut butter that has been refrigerated, warming it in the microwave may make it easier to mix into the batter.

Cider-Pecan Waffles

Makes 4 (7-inch) round Belgian waffles

These are reminiscent of the sugary, warm cider donuts that country orchards and grocers sell in the late summer and fall. Complete with melted margarine and a sprinkling of sugar, Creamy Spiced Apple Pie Sauce (page 110), or just a little hot maple syrup.

1/3 cup raw pecans, finely chopped
1 cup all-purpose flour
1 cup whole wheat flour
2 teaspoons baking powder
1 teaspoon baking soda
1 teaspoon salt
1/2 teaspoon xanthan gum powder
1/2 teaspoon ground cinnamon
1/4 teaspoon ground or grated nutmeg
1 1/2 cups apple cider
1/2 cup plus 2 tablespoons soymilk or other nondairy milk
3/4 cup sugar
1/2 cup canola oil
1 teaspoon vanilla extract

Chop the pecans and set aside. Combine the all-purpose flour, whole wheat flour, baking powder, baking soda, salt, xanthan gum powder, cinnamon, and nutmeg in a large bowl and stir with a whisk. Thoroughly mix the apple cider, soymilk, sugar, oil, and vanilla extract in a medium bowl. Pour into the flour mixture and stir just until blended. Fold in the chopped pecans.

Preheat the waffle iron for 3 to 5 minutes and spray both grids with oil. Pour or ladle the batter into the center of the iron, covering no more than two-thirds of the iron's surface for the first waffle. Adjust the amount as needed for subsequent waffles. Bake each waffle for 4 to 5 minutes, or until it can be removed easily.

Cider-Banana-Raisin Waffles (GF)

Makes 4 (7-inch) round Belgian waffles

Combining several fruit flavors, these are a bit less sugary than the Cider-Pecan Waffles (page 61), but include the natural sweetness of bananas and raisins. Serve with Banana-Maple-Nut Syrup (page 102) or vanilla soy yogurt.

1 3/4 cups brown rice flour
1/2 cup tapioca flour
2 teaspoons baking powder
1 teaspoon baking soda
1 teaspoon salt
2 teaspoons xanthan gum powder
1/2 teaspoon ground cinnamon
1 ripe banana, mashed until smooth
1 1/2 cups apple cider
3/4 cup soymilk or other nondairy milk
1/2 cup canola oil
1/2 cup sugar
1 teaspoon vanilla extract
1/3 cup raisins

Combine the rice flour, tapioca flour, baking powder, baking soda, salt, xanthan gum powder, and cinnamon in a large bowl and stir with a whisk. Mash the banana in a medium bowl, and thoroughly mix with the apple cider, soymilk, oil, sugar, and vanilla extract. Pour into the flour mixture and stir just until blended. Fold in the raisins. Let stand for 4 to 5 minutes.

Preheat the waffle iron for 3 to 5 minutes while the batter is standing. Spray both grids of the waffle iron with oil. Pour or ladle the batter into the center of the iron, covering no more than two-thirds of the iron's surface for the first waffle. Adjust the amount as needed for subsequent waffles. Bake each waffle for 4 to 6 minutes, or until it can be removed easily.

Sinful Cheesecakey Waffles

Makes 3 (7-inch) round Belgian waffles

With a light lemony flavor somewhere between a vegan cheese danish and a cheesecake, these have a dense, chewy texture. These are delicious with Amazing Amaretto Sauce (page 111), Lemon-Ginger Drizzle (page 106), strawberries, or blueberries.

> 1 cup plus 2 tablespoons all-purpose flour
> 1 1/4 teaspoons baking powder
> 1/2 teaspoon baking soda
> 3/4 teaspoon salt
> 1 1/2 teaspoons ground cinnamon
> 1 container (8 ounces) plain non-hydrogenated vegan cream cheese
> 1/2 cup soymilk or other nondairy milk
> 1/2 cup sugar
> 3 tablespoons canola oil
> 1/4 cup lemon juice
> 2 teaspoons vanilla extract

Combine the flour, baking powder, baking soda, salt, and cinnamon in a large bowl and stir with a whisk. Microwave the vegan cream cheese just until softened in a medium bowl. (This probably won't take more than 30 to 45 seconds.) Thoroughly mix the soymilk, sugar, oil, lemon juice, and vanilla extract with the vegan cream cheese. Pour into the flour mixture and stir just until blended.

Preheat the waffle iron for 3 to 5 minutes and spray both grids with oil. Pour or ladle the batter into the center of the iron, covering no more than two-thirds of the iron's surface for the first waffle. Adjust the amount as needed for subsequent waffles. Bake each waffle for 4 to 6 minutes, or until it can be removed easily.

Chocolate-Raspberry Cheesecakey Waffles

Makes 3 (7-inch) round Belgian waffles

Blending deep chocolate with tangy sweetness, these decadent desserts dance on the tongue. For an exceptional treat, top with a large dollop of Raspberry-Avocado Cream (page 102).

> 1/2 cup raspberries, fresh or defrosted to room temperature, chopped
>   into quarters
> 1 cup plus 2 tablespoons all-purpose flour
> 1/4 cup cocoa powder
> 1 1/4 teaspoons baking powder
> 1/2 teaspoon baking soda
> 3/4 teaspoon salt
> 1 container (8 ounces) plain non-hydrogenated vegan cream cheese
> 1/2 cup plus 2 tablespoons soymilk or other nondairy milk
> 1/2 cup sugar
> 1/4 cup canola oil
> 2 tablespoons lime juice
> 2 teaspoons vanilla extract

Defrost and drain the raspberries if necessary, chop them, and set aside. (If the liquid from the raspberries is flavorful, you can save it and add it to maple syrup for a topping.) Combine the flour, cocoa powder, baking powder, baking soda, and salt in a large bowl and stir with a whisk. Microwave the vegan cream cheese just until softened in a medium bowl. (This probably won't take more than 30 to 45 seconds.) Thoroughly mix the soymilk, sugar, oil, lime juice, and vanilla extract with the vegan cream cheese. Pour into the flour mixture and stir just until blended. Fold in the raspberries.

Preheat the waffle iron for 3 to 5 minutes and spray both grids with oil. Pour or ladle the batter into the center of the iron, covering no more than two-thirds of the iron's surface for the first waffle. Adjust the amount as needed for subsequent waffles. Bake each waffle for 4 to 6 minutes, or until it can be removed easily.

Chai Spice Waffles

Makes 3 (7-inch) round Belgian waffles

Chai-ching! Cash in with these high-value waffles, melding warm spices, a soothing aroma, and a dense and chewy texture. Enhance with Dark Chocolate Syrup (page 101), or top with Creamy Maple-Chai Dream Sauce (page 109) for a super chai charge.

1 cup plus 3 tablespoons all-purpose flour
1 1/4 teaspoons baking powder
1/2 teaspoon baking soda
3/4 teaspoon salt
2 teaspoons ground cinnamon
2 teaspoons ground ginger
3/4 teaspoon allspice
3/4 teaspoon ground clove
3/4 teaspoon ground or grated nutmeg
1/4 teaspoon ground cardamom (optional)
1 container (8 ounces) plain non-hydrogenated vegan cream cheese
3/4 cup soymilk or other nondairy milk
3/4 cup sugar
3 tablespoons canola oil
1 tablespoon cider vinegar
2 teaspoons vanilla extract

Combine the flour, baking powder, baking soda, salt, cinnamon, ginger, allspice, clove, nutmeg, and cardamom in a large bowl and stir with a whisk. Microwave the vegan cream cheese just until softened in a medium bowl. (This probably won't take more than 30 to 45 seconds.) Thoroughly mix the soymilk, sugar, oil, vinegar, and vanilla extract with the vegan cream cheese. Pour into the flour mixture and stir just until blended.

Preheat the waffle iron for 3 to 5 minutes and spray both grids with oil. Pour or ladle the batter into the center of the iron, covering no more than two-thirds of the iron's surface for the first waffle. Adjust the amount as needed for subsequent waffles. Bake each waffle for 4 to 5 minutes, or until it can be removed easily.

Almond-Amaranth Waffles

Makes 4 to 5 (7-inch) round Belgian waffles

These treats blend moderate sweetness with salty, toasted nuttiness. For a more pronounced and dessert-like flavor, drizzle with Amazing Amaretto Sauce (page 111) alongside the cherry halves.

> 1/2 cup raw almonds, finely chopped
> 1/4 cup plus 2 tablespoons canola oil, divided
> 1 1/2 teaspoons salt, divided
> 1 1/4 cups all-purpose flour
> 1 cup amaranth flour
> 2 teaspoons baking powder
> 1 teaspoon baking soda
> 2 1/4 cups soymilk, almond milk, or other nondairy milk
> 1/2 cup sugar
> 1/4 cup plain or vanilla soy yogurt
> 2 tablespoons ground flaxseed
> 1 1/2 teaspoons almond extract
> 1 1/2 teaspoons vanilla extract
> 1/3 cup Maraschino cherries, destemmed and chopped into halves
>   (optional, for topping)

Chop the almonds. Place them in a medium frying pan with 2 tablespoons of the oil and 1/4 teaspoon of the salt. Sauté over medium heat 4 to 5 minutes or until slightly brown, and set aside. Combine the remaining 1 1/4 teaspoons of salt, all-purpose flour, amaranth flour, baking powder, and baking soda in a large bowl and stir with a whisk. Thoroughly mix the remaining 1/4 cup of oil, soymilk, sugar, soy yogurt, flaxseed, almond extract, and vanilla extract in a medium bowl. Pour into the flour mixture and stir just until blended. Fold in the almonds.

Preheat the waffle iron for 3 to 5 minutes and spray both grids with oil. Pour or ladle the batter into the center of the iron, covering no more than two-thirds of the iron's surface for the first waffle. Adjust the amount as needed for subsequent waffles. Bake each waffle for 3 to 5 minutes, or until it can be removed easily. Top with the cherry halves.

Cashew-Carob-Molasses Waffles (GF)

Makes 4 (7-inch) round Belgian waffles

You just might become possessive after making a batch of these: "I'd better not cashew trying to eat my Cashew-Carob-Molasses Waffles!" They will touch your palate with a moderately sweet, earthy tone. Accompany with Crazeee Carob Syrup (page 102) or Maple Syrup Supreme (page 104).

1/2 cup raw cashews, finely chopped
1 1/2 cups brown rice flour
1/2 cup tapioca flour
1/2 cup roasted carob powder
2 teaspoons baking powder
1 teaspoon baking soda
1 1/4 teaspoons salt
1 1/2 teaspoons xanthan gum powder
2 cups soymilk or other nondairy milk
1/2 cup sugar
1/3 cup canola oil
1/4 cup molasses (blackstrap or other variety)
1 teaspoon vanilla extract

Chop the cashews and set aside. Combine the rice flour, tapioca flour, carob powder, baking powder, baking soda, salt, and xanthan gum powder in a large bowl and stir with a whisk. Thoroughly mix the soymilk, sugar, oil, molasses, and vanilla extract in a medium bowl. Pour into the flour mixture and stir just until blended. Fold in the cashews. Let stand for 4 to 5 minutes.

Preheat the waffle iron for 3 to 5 minutes while the batter is standing. Spray both grids of the waffle iron with oil. Pour or ladle the batter into the center of the iron, covering no more than two-thirds of the iron's surface for the first waffle. Adjust the amount as needed for subsequent waffles. Bake each waffle for 3 to 5 minutes, or until it can be removed easily.

Espresso-Key Lime Waffles

Makes 4 (7-inch) round Belgian waffles

Each of these provides a cup of perk-you-up with a sweet citrus twist. Top with additional granola, Espresso-Maple-Walnut Syrup (page 104), or Coco Kah-banana Syrup (page 105).

1 1/4 cups all-purpose flour

1 cup whole wheat flour

2 teaspoons baking powder

1 teaspoon baking soda

1 teaspoon salt

1 teaspoon xanthan gum powder

3/4 cup hot water

6 teaspoons instant espresso granules

1 cup soymilk or other nondairy milk

1 cup sugar

1/2 cup plus 2 tablespoons canola oil

1/4 cup fresh key lime juice (about 6 key limes, see note)

1 teaspoon vanilla extract

3/4 cup granola (something with maple, or your favorite type)

Combine the all-purpose flour, whole wheat flour, baking powder, baking soda, salt, and xanthan gum powder in a large bowl and stir with a whisk. Dissolve the espresso granules in the hot water in a medium bowl. The hottest water from the tap should work. Thoroughly mix the soymilk, sugar, oil, key lime juice, and vanilla extract with the dissolved coffee. Pour into the flour mixture and stir just until blended. Fold in the granola.

Preheat the waffle iron for 3 to 5 minutes and spray both grids with oil. Pour or ladle the batter into the center of the iron, covering no more than two-thirds of the iron's surface for the first waffle. Adjust the amount as needed for subsequent waffles. Bake each waffle for 3 to 4 minutes, or until it can be removed easily.

Note: You may substitute 2 tablespoons lemon juice plus 2 tablespoons regular lime juice for the key lime juice.

Mango-Chili Waffles

Makes 4 (7-inch) round Belgian waffles

MAN, these flavors GO well together. Spiciness and tangy tropical sweetness join forces to create a mouth party. Devour with vanilla soy yogurt or Very Coconutty Syrup (page 106).

    1 1/2 cups all-purpose flour
    1 cup whole wheat flour
    2 teaspoons baking powder
    1 teaspoon baking soda
    1 teaspoon salt
    2 teaspoons paprika
    1 teaspoon chili powder
    1/8 to 1/4 teaspoon ground cayenne (optional)
    2 cups soymilk or other nondairy milk
    1 ripe mango, finely chopped (about 1 cup, see note)
    3/4 cup sugar
    1/4 cup plus 2 tablespoons canola oil
    2 tablespoons lime juice
    2 teaspoons vanilla extract

Combine the all-purpose flour, whole wheat flour, baking powder, baking soda, salt, paprika, chili powder, and cayenne in a large bowl and stir with a whisk. Thoroughly mix the soymilk, mango, sugar, oil, lime juice, and vanilla extract in a medium bowl. Pour into the flour mixture and stir just until blended.

Preheat the waffle iron for 3 to 5 minutes and spray both grids with oil. Pour or ladle the batter into the center of the iron, covering no more than two-thirds of the iron's surface for the first waffle. Adjust the amount as needed for subsequent waffles. Bake each waffle for 4 to 5 minutes, or until it can be removed easily.

Note: If you don't have a fresh mango, you may substitute 1 cup of previously frozen, finely chopped mango.

Orange-Ginger Snap Waffles

Makes 4 (7-inch) round Belgian waffles

These wake up the tongue with a sugary tingle and a refreshing twist of orange. Supplement the mandarin orange bits with vegan whipped topping and candied ginger.

   1 1/2 cups all-purpose flour
   1 cup whole wheat flour
   2 teaspoons baking powder
   1 teaspoon baking soda
   1 teaspoon salt
   1 1/2 teaspoons ground ginger
   1 1/4 teaspoons ground cinnamon
   3/4 teaspoon ground clove
   1 1/4 cups soymilk or other nondairy milk
   1 cup drained mandarin orange slices, finely diced, divided
   3/4 cup sugar
   1/4 cup plus 2 tablespoons canola oil
   1/4 cup molasses (blackstrap or other variety)
   1 teaspoon orange extract
   1 teaspoon vanilla extract

Combine the all-purpose flour, whole wheat flour, baking powder, baking soda, salt, ginger, cinnamon, and clove in a large bowl and stir with a whisk. Thoroughly mix the soymilk, 1/3 cup of the mandarin orange, sugar, oil, molasses, orange extract, and vanilla extract in a medium bowl. Pour into the flour mixture and stir just until blended.

Preheat the waffle iron for 3 to 5 minutes and spray both grids with oil. Pour or ladle the batter into the center of the iron, covering no more than two-thirds of the iron's surface for the first waffle. Adjust the amount as needed for subsequent waffles. Bake each waffle for 4 to 5 minutes, or until it can be removed easily. Top the waffles with the remaining 2/3 cup of mandarin orange.

Anise Biscotti Waffles

Makes 4 (7-inch) round Belgian waffles

Fluffier and more bread-like than the crispy cafe treats, these snacks are delicious dunked in coffee, hot cocoa, tea, or Dark Chocolate Syrup (page 101).

    1/4 cup raw almonds, finely chopped
    1 cup all-purpose flour
    3/4 cup whole wheat flour
    2 teaspoons baking powder
    1 teaspoon baking soda
    3/4 teaspoon salt
    1 tablespoon plus 1 teaspoon non-ground anise seed
    1 3/4 cups soymilk or other nondairy milk
    1 cup sugar
    1/4 cup smooth applesauce
    1/4 cup canola oil
    1 1/2 teaspoons anise extract
    1 teaspoon vanilla extract

Chop the almonds and set aside. Combine the all-purpose flour, whole wheat flour, baking powder, baking soda, salt, and anise seed in a large bowl and stir with a whisk. Thoroughly mix the soymilk, sugar, applesauce, oil, anise extract, and vanilla extract in a medium bowl. Pour into the flour mixture and stir just until blended. Fold in the almonds.

Preheat the waffle iron for 3 to 5 minutes and spray both grids with oil. Pour or ladle the batter into the center of the iron, covering no more than two-thirds of the iron's surface for the first waffle. Adjust the amount as needed for subsequent waffles. Bake each waffle for 4 to 5 minutes, or until it can be removed easily.

Flavory-Savory Waffles

These waffles make heavy use of herbs, spices, and various fillings or mix-ins, alongside minimal to moderate levels of sweetness. You can enjoy them just as they are, with a very simple topping such as vegan margarine, or with the suggested toppings that complement their flavors. For example, the Refried Bean, Rice, and Cornmeal Waffles (page 79) can serve as a snack of their own, but also call out for salsa, cheese-like sauces, and vegan sour cream. The Carrot-Ginger-Sage Waffles (page 74) welcome a bit of sweetness to join the warmth and savoriness.

Spicy Blue Tortilla Chip Waffles

Makes 4 (7-inch) round Belgian waffles

Torti-yeeeah, I like these! Their taste resembles that of a spicy cheesy tortilla chip, free of the milk-based additives. Of course, they're also much fluffier and less crunchy. Eat solo or top with salsa, vegan sour cream, or black beans.

> 1 cup crumbled blue (or your favorite color) tortilla chips, broken into
> pieces smaller than a thumbnail
> 1 cup all-purpose flour
> 1/2 cup whole wheat flour
> 1/2 cup cornmeal
> 2 teaspoons baking powder
> 1 teaspoon baking soda
> 1 1/2 teaspoons salt
> 1/2 cup nutritional yeast flakes
> 1 1/2 teaspoons onion powder
> 1 1/4 teaspoons garlic powder
> 1/8 teaspoon ground cayenne
> 2 cups plus 1 tablespoon soymilk or other nondairy milk
> 1/2 cup plus 2 tablespoons canola oil
> 3 tablespoons sugar
> 2 tablespoons lime juice

Crumble the tortilla chips and set aside. Combine the all-purpose flour, whole wheat flour, cornmeal, baking powder, baking soda, salt, nutritional yeast, onion powder, garlic powder, and cayenne in a large bowl and stir with a whisk. Thoroughly mix the soymilk, oil, sugar, and lime juice in a medium bowl. Pour into the flour mixture and stir just until blended. Fold in the crumbled corn chips.

Preheat the waffle iron for 3 to 5 minutes and spray both grids with oil. Pour or ladle the batter into the center of the iron, covering no more than two-thirds of the iron's surface for the first waffle. Adjust the amount as needed for subsequent waffles. Bake each waffle for 4 to 5 minutes, or until it can be removed easily.

Carrot-Ginger-Sage Waffles

Makes 4 (7-inch) round Belgian waffles

Overtones of sage blend with just enough gingery snap to warm the palate, while carrots add another level of texture. Top with warm spoonfuls of Lemon-Ginger Drizzle (page 106) and bits of candied ginger.

1 1/4 cups grated carrots
3/4 cup all-purpose flour
3/4 cup whole wheat flour
1 1/2 teaspoons baking powder
1 teaspoon baking soda
1 teaspoon salt
1 tablespoon plus 1 teaspoon rubbed sage
1 1/2 teaspoons ground ginger
1 1/2 cups soymilk or other nondairy milk
1/4 cup plus 2 tablespoons brown sugar
1/4 cup canola oil
3 tablespoons lemon juice

Grate the carrots and set aside. Combine the all-purpose flour, whole wheat flour, baking powder, baking soda, salt, sage, and ginger in a large bowl and stir with a whisk. Thoroughly mix the carrots, soymilk, brown sugar, oil, and lemon juice in a medium bowl. Pour into the flour mixture and stir just until blended.

Preheat the waffle iron for 3 to 5 minutes and spray both grids with oil. Pour or ladle the batter into the center of the iron, covering no more than two-thirds of the iron's surface for the first waffle. Adjust the amount as needed for subsequent waffles. Bake each waffle for 3 to 5 minutes, or until it can be removed easily.

Spicy Carrot-Raisin Waffles

Makes 3 to 4 (7-inch) round Belgian waffles

Inspired by the carrot salads sometimes offered in Indian restaurants, these make for a slightly spicy-sweet treat. Garnish with spoonfuls of Mint Raita (page 120).

> 1 1/4 cups grated carrots
> 3/4 cup all-purpose flour
> 3/4 cup whole wheat flour
> 1 1/2 teaspoons baking powder
> 1 teaspoon baking soda
> 1 1/4 teaspoons salt
> 1/8 teaspoon freshly ground black pepper
> 1/8 teaspoon ground cayenne
> 1 1/4 cups plus 2 tablespoons soymilk or other nondairy milk
> 1/4 cup plus 2 tablespoons olive oil
> 1/4 cup finely chopped fresh chives
> 2 tablespoons lemon juice
> 2 tablespoons sugar
> 1/2 cup raisins

Grate the carrots and set aside. Combine the all-purpose flour, whole wheat flour, baking powder, baking soda, salt, black pepper, and cayenne in a large bowl and stir with a whisk. Thoroughly mix the carrots, soymilk, oil, chives, lemon juice, and sugar in a medium bowl. Pour into the flour mixture and stir just until blended. Fold in the raisins.

Preheat the waffle iron for 3 to 5 minutes and spray both grids with oil. Pour or ladle the batter into the center of the iron, covering no more than two-thirds of the iron's surface for the first waffle. Adjust the amount as needed for subsequent waffles. Bake each waffle for 4 to 5 minutes, or until it can be removed easily.

Orange-Basil-Cornmeal Waffles

Makes 3 to 4 (7-inch) round Belgian waffles

These sophisticated waffles blend subtle sweetness with overtones of toastedness. Top with Coconut-Cashew-Basil Sauce (page 118) or Basil-Orange Vegan Ice Cream (page 114). Because the dough needs time to rise, begin at least 3 hours in advance of baking the waffles or 1 1/2 hours in advance if you are using quick-rise yeast.

> 1 1/4 teaspoons active dry yeast
> 1 1/2 cups warm orange juice (see "Yeast-Raised Waffle Tips,"
>   page 21)
> 1 1/2 cups all-purpose flour
> 3/4 cup cornmeal
> 1 teaspoon salt
> 1/3 cup packed fresh basil, finely chopped (sweet or other variety)
> 1/4 cup plus 2 tablespoons soymilk or other nondairy milk
> 1/4 cup canola oil
> 1/4 cup sugar
> 1 1/2 teaspoons baking powder
> 1 teaspoon vanilla extract

Dissolve the yeast in the warm orange juice in a large non-metal bowl. Let stand for 5 minutes. Stir in the all-purpose flour, cornmeal, and salt until well blended. Cover the bowl and place it in a warm location until the flour mixture has almost doubled (see "Yeast-Raised Waffle Tips," page 21).

After the flour mixture has risen, combine the basil, soymilk, oil, sugar, baking powder, and vanilla extract in a medium bowl. Thoroughly mix, breaking up any clumps of baking powder. Pour into the raised flour mixture and stir until well blended. Let stand for 15 minutes.

Preheat the waffle iron for 3 to 5 minutes while the batter is standing. Spray both grids of the waffle iron with oil. Pour or ladle the batter into the center of the iron, covering no more than two-thirds of the iron's surface for the first waffle. Adjust the amount as needed for subsequent waffles. Bake each waffle for 4 to 6 minutes, or until it can be removed easily.

Cheddar Cheesy Waffles

Makes 4 (7-inch) round Belgian waffles

Suited for a snack or a meal, these are reminiscent of savory and salty cheese-flavored crackers—except they're vegan and 100 times as large. Serve solo, with Southwestern Beans and Greens (page 122), or with applesauce.

> 1 cup all-purpose flour
> 1/2 cup whole wheat flour
> 1/2 cup rolled oats
> 2 teaspoons baking powder
> 1 teaspoon baking soda
> 3/4 teaspoon salt (see note)
> 3 tablespoons nutritional yeast flakes
> 1 teaspoon onion powder
> 1/2 teaspoon paprika
> 1/4 teaspoon garlic powder
> 1/4 teaspoon dry mustard powder
> 2 cups soymilk or other nondairy milk
> 1/4 cup canola oil
> 2 tablespoons sugar
> 2 tablespoons fresh lemon juice
> 1 tablespoon plus 2 teaspoons light or chickpea miso
> 1 tablespoon prepared horseradish (optional)

Combine the all-purpose flour, whole wheat flour, oats, baking powder, baking soda, salt, nutritional yeast, onion powder, paprika, garlic powder, and mustard powder in a large bowl and stir with a whisk. Thoroughly mix the soymilk, oil, sugar, lemon juice, miso, and horseradish in a medium bowl. Break up any clumps of miso. Pour into the flour mixture and stir just until blended. Let stand for 4 to 5 minutes.

Preheat the waffle iron for 3 to 5 minutes while the batter is standing. Spray both grids of the waffle iron with oil. Pour or ladle the batter into the center of the iron, covering no more than two-thirds of the iron's surface for the first waffle. Adjust the amount as needed for subsequent waffles. Bake each waffle for 4 to 5 minutes, or until it can be removed easily.

Refried Bean & Cornmeal Waffles

Makes 5 (7-inch) round Belgian waffles

Have you ever wondered what might happen if you tried to combine a whole Mexican meal in a waffle iron? Lime, cumin, and cayenne lend a south of the border style. Top with salsa, guacamole, vegan sour cream, and vegan cheese.

> 3/4 cup all-purpose flour
> 3/4 cup whole wheat flour
> 3/4 cup cornmeal
> 2 teaspoons baking powder
> 1 teaspoon baking soda
> 1 teaspoon salt (see note)
> 1 3/4 teaspoons ground cumin
> 1 teaspoon onion powder
> 1/8 teaspoon ground cayenne
> 1 1/2 cups soymilk or other nondairy milk
> 1 can (15 ounces) refried black beans
> 1/4 cup plus 2 tablespoons canola oil
> 3 tablespoons lime juice
> 3 tablespoons sugar

Combine the all-purpose flour, whole wheat flour, cornmeal, baking powder, baking soda, salt, cumin, onion powder, and cayenne in a large bowl and stir with a whisk. Thoroughly mix the soymilk, beans, oil, lime juice, and sugar in a medium bowl. Pour into the flour mixture and stir just until blended.

Preheat the waffle iron for 3 to 5 minutes and spray both grids with oil. Pour or ladle the batter into the center of the iron, covering no more than two-thirds of the iron's surface for the first waffle. Adjust the amount as needed for subsequent waffles. Bake each waffle for 4 to 6 minutes, or until it can be removed easily.

Note: You may reduce the salt to 3/4 teaspoon or less if using refried beans that are already heavily salted.

Refried Bean, Rice, & Cornmeal Waffles (GF)

Makes 5 (7-inch) round Belgian waffles

These are a bit lighter and crispier than the Refried Bean and Cornmeal Waffles (page 78). Salsa, guacamole, vegan sour cream, and vegan cheese remain the perfect match for the subtle citrus and warm spices.

1 1/4 cups brown or white rice flour
1/2 cup tapioca flour
3/4 cup cornmeal
2 teaspoons baking powder
1 teaspoon baking soda
1 teaspoon salt (see note)
1 3/4 teaspoons xanthan gum powder
1 3/4 teaspoons ground cumin
1 teaspoon onion powder
1/8 teaspoon ground cayenne
1 1/2 cups soymilk or other nondairy milk
1 can (15 ounces) refried black beans
1/4 cup plus 2 tablespoons canola oil
3 tablespoons lime juice
3 tablespoons sugar

Combine the rice flour, tapioca flour, cornmeal, baking powder, baking soda, salt, xanthan gum powder, cumin, onion powder, and cayenne in a large bowl and stir with a whisk. Thoroughly mix the soymilk, beans, oil, lime juice, and sugar in a medium bowl. Pour into the flour mixture and stir just until blended. Let stand for 3 to 4 minutes.

Preheat the waffle iron for 3 to 5 minutes while the batter is standing. Spray both grids of the waffle iron with oil. Pour or ladle the batter into the center of the iron, covering no more than two-thirds of the iron's surface for the first waffle. Adjust the amount as needed for subsequent waffles. Bake each waffle for 4 to 6 minutes, or until it can be removed easily.

Note: You may reduce the salt to 3/4 teaspoon or less if using refried beans that are already heavily salted.

Banana-Fofana-Walnut Waffles

Makes 4 (7-inch) round Belgian waffles

The airy texture of spelt is married to gentle spice and sweetness. I sometimes dream about these waffles and wake up gnawing on the corner of my pillow. They make great partners for Banana-Maple-Nut Syrup (page 102) or just warm maple syrup.

1/3 cup raw finely chopped walnuts
1 3/4 cups spelt flour
1/2 cup rolled oats
2 teaspoons baking powder
3/4 teaspoon salt
1 1/2 teaspoons ground cinnamon
3/4 teaspoon ground or grated nutmeg
1/2 teaspoon ground ginger
1 ripe banana, mashed until smooth
2 1/4 cups soymilk or other nondairy milk
3 tablespoons canola oil
2 tablespoons ground flaxseed
1 teaspoon vanilla extract

Chop the walnuts and set aside. Combine the flour, oats, baking powder, salt, cinnamon, nutmeg, and ginger in a large bowl and stir with a whisk. Mash the banana in a medium bowl, and thoroughly mix with the soymilk, oil, flaxseed, and vanilla extract. Pour into the flour mixture and stir just until blended. Fold in the walnuts. Let stand for 6 to 7 minutes.

Preheat the waffle iron for 3 to 5 minutes while the batter is standing. Spray both grids of the waffle iron with oil. Pour or ladle the batter into the center of the iron, covering no more than two-thirds of the iron's surface for the first waffle. Adjust the amount as needed for subsequent waffles. Bake each waffle for 4 to 5 minutes, or until it can be removed easily.

Umami Mama Waffles: The Mother of Savory

Makes 4 (7-inch) round Belgian waffles

This isn't the name of an Abba musical, but these pizza-like waffles should make your taste buds sing. Savor them as they are, or create perfect harmony with the Savory Cashew-Mushroom Sauce (page 117). Because the dough needs time to rise, begin at least 3 hours in advance of baking the waffles or 1 1/2 hours in advance if you are using quick-rise yeast.

> 1 1/4 teaspoons active dry yeast
> 1 1/2 cups warm water
> 1 cup all-purpose flour
> 1 cup whole wheat flour
> 3/4 teaspoon salt
> 1/3 cup pitted and finely chopped Kalamata olives
> 1/3 cup finely chopped sun-dried tomatoes, preserved in olive oil or rehydrated
> 1 cup soymilk or other nondairy milk
> 1/4 cup olive oil
> 3 tablespoons nutritional yeast flakes
> 1 tablespoon plus 1 teaspoon light or chickpea miso
> 1 tablespoon ground flaxseed
> 1 tablespoon sugar
> 2 medium cloves garlic, crushed
> 1 teaspoon baking powder
> 1 teaspoon dried basil
> 1 teaspoon onion powder
> 1 teaspoon dried oregano
> 1/8 to 1/4 teaspoon ground cayenne

Dissolve the yeast in the water in a large non-metal bowl. Let stand for 5 minutes. Stir in the all-purpose flour, whole wheat flour, and salt until well blended. Cover the bowl and place it in a warm location until the flour mixture has almost doubled (see "Yeast-Raised Waffle Tips," page 21).

After the flour mixture has risen, chop the olives and sun-dried tomatoes, and set aside. Combine the soymilk, oil, nutritional yeast, miso, flaxseed, sugar, garlic, baking powder, basil, onion powder, oregano, and cayenne in a medium bowl. Mix thoroughly, breaking up any clumps of miso. Pour into the raised flour mixture and stir until well blended. Fold in the olives and sun-dried tomatoes, and let stand for 15 minutes.

Preheat the waffle iron for 3 to 5 minutes while the batter is standing. Spray both grids of the waffle iron with oil. Pour or ladle the batter into the center of the iron, covering no more than two-thirds of the iron's surface for the first waffle. Adjust the amount as needed for subsequent waffles. Bake each waffle for 4 to 6 minutes, or until it can be removed easily.

Caramelized Onion & Garlic Waffles

Makes 3 to 4 (7-inch) round Belgian waffles

This is a classic flavor combination, adapted to the exciting world of vegan waffles. Top with You Make Miso Tangy Dipping Sauce (page 119), pizza sauce, or melted vegan cheese. Because the dough needs time to rise, begin at least 3 hours in advance of baking the waffles or 1 1/2 hours in advance if you are using quick-rise yeast.

1 1/4 teaspoons active dry yeast
1 1/2 cups warm water
1 cup all-purpose flour
1 cup whole wheat flour
1 1/2 teaspoons salt
1 cup chopped onion
3 medium cloves garlic, crushed
1/4 cup plus 2 tablespoons olive oil, divided
1/4 cup plus 2 tablespoons soymilk or other nondairy milk
2 tablespoons plain soy yogurt
2 tablespoons sugar
1/2 teaspoon baking powder
1/2 teaspoon baking soda
1/4 teaspoon freshly ground black pepper
1/8 teaspoon ground cayenne

Dissolve the yeast in the water in a large non-metal bowl. Let stand for 5 minutes. Stir in the all-purpose flour, whole wheat flour, and salt until well blended. Cover the bowl and place it in a warm location until the flour mixture has almost doubled (see "Yeast-Raised Waffle Tips," page 21).

After the flour mixture has risen, chop the onion. Combine it with the garlic and 2 tablespoons of the oil in a medium frying pan. Sauté over medium heat for about 5 minutes, or until the onions have softened and the garlic has started to brown. Remove from heat and set aside.

Combine the remaining 1/4 cup of oil, soymilk, soy yogurt, sugar, baking powder, baking soda, black pepper, and cayenne in a medium bowl. Mix thoroughly, breaking up any clumps of baking powder or baking soda. Pour into the raised flour mixture and stir until well blended. Fold in the onions and garlic. Let stand for 15 minutes.

Preheat the waffle iron for 3 to 5 minutes while the batter is standing. Spray both grids of the waffle iron with oil. Pour or ladle the batter into the center of the iron, covering no more than two-thirds of the iron's surface for the first waffle. Adjust the amount as needed for subsequent waffles. Bake each waffle for 4 to 6 minutes, or until it can be removed easily.

Chili-Lime Felafel Waffles

Makes 3 (7-inch) dense round Belgian waffles

Like traditional felafel, these are dense and filling with a bit of a kick; but they incorporate a slight twist in spices. Top with tomatoes, cucumbers, and Cilantro-Lime Tahini Sauce (page 118), and serve on a bed of leafy greens.

> 2 cans (15 ounces each) chickpeas, rinsed and drained (about 3 cups)
> 1/2 cup whole wheat or all-purpose flour
> 1/4 cup plus 2 tablespoons lime juice
> 1/4 cup plus 2 tablespoons olive oil
> 1/4 cup water
> 4 medium cloves garlic
> 2 tablespoons sugar
> 1 tablespoon chili powder
> 2 teaspoons ground cumin
> 1 teaspoon ground coriander
> 1 teaspoon onion powder
> 1 teaspoon salt
> 1 teaspoon xanthan gum powder
> 1/8 to 1/4 teaspoon ground cayenne
> 1 1/2 teaspoons baking powder
> 1 teaspoon baking soda

Place all the ingredients into a food processor or powerful blender, adding the baking powder and baking soda last. Process until smooth or until few small clumps remain (see note).

Preheat the waffle iron for 3 to 5 minutes and spray both grids with oil. Pour or ladle the batter into the center of the iron, covering no more than two-thirds of the iron's surface for the first waffle. Adjust the amount as needed for subsequent waffles. Bake each waffle for 4 to 6 minutes, or until it can be removed easily.

Note: You may need to process the batter in 2 or 3 smaller portions and then stir them together by hand, especially if using a blender.

Spanakowafflita

Makes 4 (7-inch) round Belgian waffles

Spanako-what? Don't worry about the name because it's not good to talk with a full mouth anyway. These are reminiscent of the spanakopita or spinach pies often served at Greek food festivals, minus the dairy. They can be eaten as a main course for lunch or dinner, and they blend well with the Savory Cashew-Mushroom Sauce (page 117).

> 2 1/2 cups packed fresh spinach, finely chopped (see note)
> 1/2 cup packed fresh parsley, finely chopped (see note)
> 3 green onions, finely chopped (use entire onion)
> 1 1/2 cups whole wheat flour
> 1/2 cup all-purpose flour
> 2 teaspoons baking powder
> 1 teaspoon baking soda
> 3/4 teaspoon salt
> 1 teaspoon onion powder
> 1/8 teaspoon ground cayenne
> 2 cups soymilk or other nondairy milk
> 1/4 cup olive oil
> 2 tablespoons light or chickpea miso
> 1 tablespoon ground flaxseed
> 1 tablespoon sugar
> 1 tablespoon white or red wine vinegar
> 2 medium cloves garlic, crushed

Chop the spinach, parsley, and onions, and set aside. Combine the whole wheat flour, all-purpose flour, baking powder, baking soda, salt, onion powder, and cayenne in a large bowl and stir with a whisk. Thoroughly mix the soymilk, oil, miso, flaxseed, sugar, vinegar, and garlic in a medium bowl. Break up any clumps of miso. Pour into the flour mixture and stir just until blended. Fold in the chopped spinach, parsley, and onions.

Preheat the waffle iron for 3 to 5 minutes and spray both grids with oil. Pour or ladle the batter into the center of the iron, covering no more than two-thirds of the iron's surface for the first waffle. Adjust the amount as needed for subsequent waffles. Bake each waffle for 5 to 6 minutes, or until it can be removed easily.

Note: The spinach and parsley should be chopped into pieces no larger than a thumbnail. If they are not chopped finely enough, the waffles will be more likely to separate in the middle upon opening the iron. As an emergency measure, you can add 1/4 to 1/2 teaspoon xanthan gum powder.

Kale-idoscopic Waffles

Makes 4 (7-inch) round Belgian waffles

Staring at a round waffle is somewhat like looking into a kaleidoscope, because the 4 quadrants are nearly mirror images of one another. Don't spend too much time gazing at one of these, though, because it is tastiest while it's hot. A peanutty-salty-spicy blend accents bits of nutritious green kale. Top with Simple Piña Colada-ish Topping (page 110), bits of juicy pineapple, or slices of sautéed onion.

> 3 cups packed fresh kale, leaf stems removed before measuring, finely chopped (any variety, also see note)
> 1 1/2 cups whole wheat flour
> 1/2 cup all-purpose flour
> 2 teaspoons baking powder
> 1/2 teaspoon baking soda
> 1/4 teaspoon salt
> 1 1/2 teaspoons onion powder
> 1/4 teaspoon ground cayenne
> 2 1/4 cups soymilk or other nondairy milk
> 1/2 cup smooth peanut butter, salted (see note)
> 3 tablespoons brown sugar
> 2 tablespoons ground flaxseed
> 3 tablespoons soy sauce
> 2 medium cloves garlic, crushed

Chop the kale and set aside. Combine the whole wheat flour, all-purpose flour, baking powder, baking soda, salt, onion powder, and cayenne in a large bowl and stir with a whisk. Thoroughly mix the soymilk, peanut butter, brown sugar, flaxseed, soy sauce, and garlic in a medium bowl. Break up any clumps of peanut butter. Pour into the flour mixture and stir just until blended. Fold in the kale. Let stand for 3 to 4 minutes.

Preheat the waffle iron for 3 to 5 minutes while the batter is standing. Spray both grids of the waffle iron with oil. Pour or ladle the batter into the center of the iron, covering no more than two-thirds of the iron's surface for the first waffle. Adjust the amount as needed for subsequent waffles. Bake each waffle for 4 to 5 minutes, or until it can be removed easily.

Note: The kale should be chopped into pieces no larger than your thumbnail. If it is not chopped finely enough, the waffles will be more likely to separate in the middle upon opening the iron.

Note: If you're using peanut butter that has been refrigerated, warming it in the microwave may make it easier to mix into the batter.

Avocado-Pecan Waffles for Two

Makes 2 (7-inch) round Belgian waffles

The subtle but delicious flavors in these waffles go best with plain or vanilla soy yogurt, applesauce, or Raspberry-Avocado Cream (page 102). Enjoy with a friend, or eat both if you're extra hungry.

 1/4 cup finely chopped raw pecans
 3/4 cup all-purpose flour
 1/4 cup whole wheat flour
 1 1/4 teaspoon baking powder
 1/2 teaspoon baking soda
 1/2 teaspoon salt
 1/4 teaspoon ground or grated nutmeg
 1 ripe avocado, mashed until smooth (Hass or other variety)
 1/2 cup soymilk or other nondairy milk
 1/4 cup plus 1 tablespoon sugar
 1/4 cup water
 2 tablespoons canola oil
 2 tablespoons lime juice

Chop the pecans and set aside. Combine the all-purpose flour, whole wheat flour, baking powder, baking soda, salt, and nutmeg in a large bowl and stir with a whisk. Mash the avocado in a medium bowl, and thoroughly mix with the soymilk, sugar, water, oil, and lime juice. Pour into the flour mixture and stir just until blended. Fold in the pecans.

Preheat the waffle iron for 3 to 5 minutes and spray both grids with oil. Pour or ladle the batter into the center of the iron, covering no more than two-thirds of the iron's surface for the first waffle. Adjust the amount as needed for subsequent waffles. Bake each waffle for 4 to 5 minutes, or until it can be removed easily.

Yeast-Raised Cornmeal Chili-Dippin' Waffles

Makes 4 (7-inch) round Belgian waffles.

These crispy waffles have a subtler sweetness than the average cornbread, with the uncommon addition of sourdough-like overtones. Because the dough needs time to rise, begin at least 3 hours in advance of baking the waffles or 1 1/2 hours in advance if you are using quick-rise yeast. Along with chili, these blend well with the Spicy Sloppy Tofu and Portabella (page 124) or the Southwestern Beans and Greens (page 122).

> 1 1/4 teaspoons active dry yeast
> 1 1/2 cups warm water (see "Yeast-Raised Waffle Tips," page 21)
> 3/4 cup all-purpose flour
> 1/2 cup whole wheat flour
> 3/4 cup cornmeal
> 1 1/2 teaspoons salt
> 1/2 cup soymilk or other nondairy milk
> 1/4 cup plus 2 tablespoons canola oil
> 1/4 cup brown sugar
> 2 tablespooons molasses (blackstrap or other variety)
> 1/2 teaspoon baking powder
> 1/2 teaspoon baking soda

Dissolve the yeast in the water in a large non-metal bowl. Let stand for 5 minutes. Stir in the all-purpose flour, whole wheat flour, cornmeal, and salt until well blended. Cover the bowl and place it in a warm location until the flour mixture has almost doubled (see "Yeast-Raised Waffle Tips," page 21).

After the flour mixture has risen, combine the soymilk, oil, brown sugar, molasses, baking powder, and baking soda in a small bowl. Mix thoroughly, breaking up any clumps of baking powder or baking soda. Pour into the raised flour mixture and stir until well blended. Let stand for 15 minutes.

Preheat the waffle iron for 3 to 5 minutes while the batter is standing. Spray both grids of the waffle iron with oil. Pour or ladle the batter into the center of the iron, covering no more than two-thirds of the iron's surface for the first waffle. Adjust the amount as needed for subsequent waffles. Bake each waffle for 3 to 5 minutes, or until it can be removed easily.

Quinoa-Full Keen Waffles

Makes 4 (7-inch) round Belgian waffles

This waffle sports 2 different textures of an ancient super seed, with the chewiness and occasional crunch of whole quinoa adding texture and contrast. Drizzle with warm almond butter or maple syrup.

> 1/4 cup plus 2 tablespoons quinoa seed (also called quinoa grain; see note)
> 1/4 cup plus 3 tablespoons water
> 1/2 cup plus 1 teaspoon canola oil, divided
> 1 1/2 cups quinoa flour
> 1/2 cup tapioca flour
> 2 teaspoons baking powder
> 1 teaspoon baking soda
> 1 teaspoon salt
> 3/4 teaspoon xanthan gum powder
> 1/2 teaspoon ground cinnamon
> 1/2 teaspoon ground or grated nutmeg
> 2 cups soymilk or other nondairy milk
> 1/4 cup plus 2 tablespoons maple syrup
> 1/4 cup raisins

Place the quinoa seed in a small saucepan with the water and 1 teaspoon of the oil. Cover and heat just until boiling. Then stir, reduce heat, and simmer covered for another 10 minutes. Turn off heat and let stand covered for 5 minutes.

While the quinoa seed is simmering or standing, combine the quinoa flour, tapioca flour, baking powder, baking soda, salt, xanthan gum powder, cinnamon, and nutmeg in a large bowl and stir with a whisk. Thoroughly mix the remaining 1/2 cup of oil, soymilk, and maple syrup in a medium bowl. Pour into the flour mixture and stir just until blended. Fold in the cooked quinoa seed and the raisins.

Preheat the waffle iron for 3 to 5 minutes and spray both grids with oil. Pour or ladle the batter into the center of the iron, covering no more than two-thirds of the iron's surface for the first waffle. Adjust the amount as needed for subsequent waffles. Bake each waffle for 4 to 5 minutes, or until it can be removed easily.

Note: Prior to cooking, place a few pieces of the whole quinoa seed on your tongue. If you detect a strong bitterness, follow the suggestions under "Quinoa Seed and Flour" (page 24).

Keen Zucchini-Dill Waffles

Makes 4 (7-inch) round Belgian waffles

When midsummer brings an abundance of fresh zucchini, just make waffles out of them. The dill adds to the refreshing zucchini flavor, and the cashews provide richness. Top with plain or vanilla soy yogurt and a twist of lemon juice.

1 1/2 cups grated zucchini
1/2 cup raw cashews, finely chopped
1/4 cup plus 2 tablespoons fresh dill leaves, finely chopped
1 cup all-purpose flour
1 cup whole wheat flour
2 teaspoons baking powder
1 teaspoon baking soda
1 1/2 teaspoons salt
2 tablespoons nutritional yeast flakes
1/2 teaspoon freshly ground black pepper
1 3/4 cups soymilk or other nondairy milk
1/4 cup plus 2 tablespoons canola oil
1/4 cup plus 2 tablespoons sugar
2 tablespoons lemon juice

Grate the zucchini, chop the cashews, chop the dill, and set them aside. Combine the all-purpose flour, whole wheat flour, baking powder, baking soda, salt, nutritional yeast, and pepper in a large bowl and stir with a whisk. Thoroughly mix the zucchini, dill, soymilk, oil, sugar, and lemon juice in a medium bowl. Pour into the flour mixture and stir just until blended. Fold in the cashews.

Preheat the waffle iron for 3 to 5 minutes and spray both grids with oil. Pour or ladle the batter into the center of the iron, covering no more than two-thirds of the iron's surface for the first waffle. Adjust the amount as needed for subsequent waffles. Bake each waffle for 4 to 6 minutes, or until it can be removed easily.

Some Awesome Samosa Waffles

Makes 4 (7-inch) round Belgian waffles

These are a tribute to the flavorfully stuffed pastry pockets served at Indian restaurants. Raisins add modest sweetness to a tongue-tingling combination of spices. Enjoy with a few spoonfuls of Mint Raita (page 120).

> 1 cup peeled, cooked, drained and thoroughly mashed potatoes, no
>   liquid added (roughly 2 medium potatoes)
> 1/2 cup peas (defrosted to room temperature and drained, if
>   previously frozen)
> 2 tablespoons finely chopped raw cashews
> 1 cup whole wheat flour
> 1/2 cup all-purpose flour
> 2 teaspoons baking powder
> 1 teaspoon baking soda
> 1 1/4 teaspoons salt
> 2 teaspoons ground coriander
> 1 1/2 teaspoons garam masala powder
> 1 teaspoon ground ginger
> 1 teaspoon onion powder
> 2 cups soymilk or other nondairy milk
> 1/4 cup canola oil
> 3 tablespoons sugar
> 2 tablespoons lemon juice
> 1 medium clove garlic, crushed
> 2 tablespoons raisins

Place the potatoes in a pot of boiling water or in the microwave, cooking them until they're soft enough to mash easily. While the potatoes are cooking, defrost and drain the peas if necessary, and set aside. Chop the cashews and set aside. Combine the whole wheat flour, all-purpose flour, baking powder, baking soda, salt, coriander, garam masala, ginger, and onion powder in a large bowl and stir with a whisk.

After the potatoes are soft, drain them and mash them until all lumps are gone. Measure 1 cup of the mashed potatoes into a medium bowl and

95

thoroughly mix with the soymilk, oil, sugar, lemon juice, and garlic. Pour into the flour mixture and stir just until blended. Fold in the peas, cashews, and raisins.

Preheat the waffle iron for 3 to 5 minutes and spray both grids with oil. Pour or ladle the batter into the center of the iron, covering no more than two-thirds of the iron's surface for the first waffle. Adjust the amount as needed for subsequent waffles. Bake each waffle for 4 to 5 minutes, or until it can be removed easily.

Mucho Molassesey Vegan Power Waffles (GF)

Makes 4 (7-inch) round Belgian waffles

Great for the physically active waffler, these pack more potassium and protein than the average waffle. Their strong molasses flavor is not for the faint of heart, especially if blackstrap molasses is used. Top with chocolate or carob chips, or Maple Syrup Supreme (page 104).

1 3/4 cups brown rice flour
1/2 cup tapioca flour
1/2 cup hemp powder (ground hempseed)
2 teaspoons baking powder
1 teaspoon baking soda
1 teaspoon salt
1 teaspoon xanthan gum powder
1/2 teaspoon ground cinnamon (optional)
2 ripe bananas, mashed until smooth
2 1/4 cups soymilk or other nondairy milk
1/4 cup plus 2 tablespoons canola oil
1/4 cup plus 2 tablespoons molasses (blackstrap or other variety)
1 teaspoon vanilla extract

Combine the rice flour, tapioca flour, hemp powder, baking powder, baking soda, salt, xanthan gum powder, and cinnamon in a large bowl and stir with a whisk. Mash the bananas in a medium bowl, and thoroughly mix with the soymilk, oil, molasses, and vanilla extract. Pour into the flour mixture and stir just until blended. Let stand for 3 to 4 minutes.

Preheat the waffle iron for 3 to 5 minutes while the batter is standing. Spray both grids of the waffle iron with oil. Pour or ladle the batter into the center of the iron, covering no more than two-thirds of the iron's surface for the first waffle. Adjust the amount as needed for subsequent waffles. Bake each waffle for 4 to 5 minutes, or until it can be removed easily.

Sesame Waffles

Makes 4 (7-inch) round Belgian waffles

Remember the secret phrase for entry to the waffle party: "Open, iron with sesame waffle!" A bit on the sweeter side of savory, these are light and slightly crispy, with additional texture from the seeds. Warm maple syrup or Lemon-Ginger Drizzle (page 106) creates a delicious combination.

> 3/4 cup all-purpose flour
> 3/4 cup whole wheat flour
> 2 teaspoons baking powder
> 1 teaspoon baking soda
> 1 1/4 teaspoon salt
> 1/2 cup toasted sesame seeds (white or black)
> 1 1/2 cups plus 2 tablespoons soymilk or other nondairy milk
> 1/2 cup sugar
> 1/2 cup tahini (sesame seed butter)
> 1/4 cup canola oil
> 2 tablespoons ground flaxseed
> 2 tablespoons lemon juice

Combine the all-purpose flour, whole wheat flour, baking powder, baking soda, salt, and sesame seeds in a large bowl and stir with a whisk. Thoroughly mix the soymilk, sugar, tahini, oil, flaxseed, and lemon juice in a medium bowl. Pour into the flour mixture and stir just until blended.

Preheat the waffle iron for 3 to 5 minutes and spray both grids with oil. Pour or ladle the batter into the center of the iron, covering no more than two-thirds of the iron's surface for the first waffle. Adjust the amount as needed for subsequent waffles. Bake each waffle for 3 to 4 minutes, or until it can be removed easily.

Flavory-Sweet Waffle Toppings

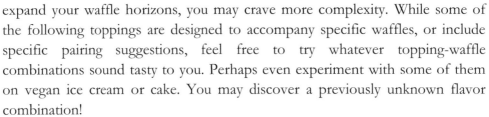

You may often be in the mood for a waffle with a warm drizzle of maple syrup or some fresh slices of colorful fruit on top. There's certainly nothing wrong with that. However, as you expand your waffle horizons, you may crave more complexity. While some of the following toppings are designed to accompany specific waffles, or include specific pairing suggestions, feel free to try whatever topping-waffle combinations sound tasty to you. Perhaps even experiment with some of them on vegan ice cream or cake. You may discover a previously unknown flavor combination!

Dark Chocolate Syrup & Variations

Makes about 3/4 cup

This has a deeper and more bittersweet chocolate flavor than most store-bought chocolate syrups. It complements strawberries and other fresh fruit toppings, as well as vegan ice cream. Enjoy with PBMax Waffles (page 60) or Cider-Pecan Waffles (page 61).

> 1/2 cup sugar
> 1/4 cup plus 1 tablespoon cocoa powder
> 1/4 cup vegan margarine
> 1/4 cup soymilk or other nondairy milk
> 1 teaspoon vanilla extract

Combine all the ingredients except the vanilla extract in a small saucepan. Stir briskly and constantly over medium heat until half a minute after it begins to boil. Continue to scrape the bottom to incorporate any dry cocoa and keep it from burning. Immediately remove from heat and stir in the vanilla extract.

Dark Chocolate Amaretto Syrup: Add 2 or 3 tablespoons of amaretto after turning off heat.

Dark Chocolate Orangalicious Syrup: Add 1 teaspoon of orange extract after turning off heat.

Dark Chocolate Peebee Syrup: Add 1/4 cup smooth or chunky peanut butter before heating. Other nut butters, such as cashew or almond, can also provide an extra-rich flavor.

South of the Border Dark Chocolate Syrup: Add 1 teaspoon of ground cinnamon and 1/8 teaspoon of ground cayenne before heating.

Crazeee Carob Syrup

Makes about 3/4 cup

This provides a complex dimension of richness different from that of the Dark Chocolate Syrup (page 101). Drizzle atop Mucho Molassesey Vegan Power Waffles (page 97).

> 1/3 cup roasted carob powder
> 1/3 cup sugar
> 1/4 cup vegan margarine
> 1/4 cup soymilk or other nondairy milk
> 1 teaspoon vanilla extract

Combine all the ingredients except the vanilla extract in a small saucepan. Stir briskly and constantly over medium heat until half a minute after it begins to boil. Immediately remove from heat and stir in the vanilla extract.

Note: For variation ideas, see variations for Dark Chocolate Syrup (page 101).

Banana-Maple-Nut Syrup

Makes 3/4 cup

This textured, salty-sweet accompaniment meshes well with the Banana-Fofana-Walnut Waffles (page 80) or the Banana-Blueberry-Teff Waffles (page 55).

> 1 ripe banana, mashed until smooth
> 1/4 cup maple syrup
> 1/4 cup pecans or walnuts, finely chopped
> 1/8 teaspoon salt (reduce or omit if nuts are already salted)

Mash the banana in a small saucepan, and mix with the maple syrup, nuts, and salt. Stir constantly over medium heat, just until warm.

Cocoa or Carob Agave Nectar

Makes about 1 cup

This decadent sauce takes the Dark Chocolate Syrup (page 101) and Crazeee Carob Syrup (page 102) in yet another direction with molasses overtones. Pour over Dark Chocolate Cake Waffles (page 57) or Cashew-Carob-Molasses Waffles (page 67) and vegan ice cream for a deep, dark, delicious dessert.

1/2 cup agave nectar
1/4 cup plus 1 tablespoon cocoa powder
1/4 cup plus 1 tablespoon molasses (blackstrap or other variety)
1/4 cup vegan margarine
1 teaspoon vanilla extract

Combine all the ingredients except the vanilla extract in a small saucepan. Stir constantly over medium heat just until it begins to boil, the margarine is entirely melted, and the cocoa and sugar are well dissolved. Immediately remove from heat and stir in the vanilla extract.

Carob Agave Nectar: Replace the cocoa powder with 1/4 cup plus 2 tablespoons of roasted carob powder.

Espresso-Maple-Walnut Syrup

Makes 1 cup

Nuts, maple, and additional espresso zing enhance the Espresso-Key Lime Waffles (page 68) or the Banana-Fofana-Walnut Waffles (page 80).

> 1/4 cup walnuts, finely chopped
> 1 teaspoon instant espresso granules
> 2 tablespoons hot water
> 1/4 cup maple syrup
> 1/4 cup plain or vanilla soy yogurt
> 1 tablespoon brown sugar
> 1 tablespoon vegan margarine
> 1/8 teaspoon salt

Chop the walnuts and set aside. Dissolve the espresso granules in the hot water in a small saucepan. (The hottest water from the tap should work.) Add the maple syrup, soy yogurt, brown sugar, margarine, salt, and walnuts. Stir constantly over medium heat until the margarine is melted.

Maple Syrup Supreme

Makes 1 1/4 cups

If you love maple syrup and desire a fuller and more complex flavor, this is sure to please. Generously ladle onto the Pass the Buckwheat-Oat Waffles (page 44) or the Crispy Maple-Cashew Waffles (page 56).

> 3/4 cup maple syrup
> 1/4 cup vegan margarine
> 1/4 cup molasses (blackstrap or other variety)

Combine all the ingredients in a small saucepan. Stir constantly over medium heat until the margarine is melted and the mixture just begins to boil.

Coco Kah-banana Syrup

Makes 1 to 1 1/4 cups

For coffee flavor with a tropical twist, place this atop the Espresso-Key Lime Waffles (page 68). It also plays well with the Dark Chocolate Cake Waffles (page 57).

> **1 ripe banana, mashed until smooth**
> **1/2 cup coconut milk (not the "light" variety)**
> **1/4 cup Kahlua or other coffee-flavored liqueur (see note for alcohol-free version)**
> **1/4 cup sugar**

Mash the banana in a small bowl, and mix with the coconut milk, Kahlua, and sugar until the sugar is dissolved.

Note: For an alcohol-free version, omit liqueur, add 2 teaspoons instant coffee granules dissolved in 1/4 cup of warm water, and increase sugar by 1 tablespoon.

Very Coconutty Syrup

Makes about 1 cup

Coconutty is oh-so-nutty. This blend embellishes the Mango-Chili Waffles (page 69) or adds a super coconuttiness to the Coconut-Date Waffles (page 59).

1/4 cup coconut, shredded unsweetened (macaroon style)
1/4 cup coconut milk (not the "light" variety)
1/4 cup plain or vanilla soy yogurt (see note)
1/4 cup sugar
2 tablespoons water
1/2 teaspoon vanilla extract

Combine all the ingredients in a small bowl and mix until the sugar is dissolved.

Note: If you'd like the topping even sweeter and even more coconutty, omit the soy yogurt. This will yield about 3/4 cup.

Lemon-Ginger Drizzle

Makes 1 1/4 cups

Tart and sweet with the added warmth of ginger, this sauce provides a flavorful accent to the Carrot-Ginger-Sage Waffles (page 74) or the Generously Ginger-Lemon-Chocolate Waffles (page 54).

1/2 cup vegan margarine
1/2 cup soymilk or other nondairy milk
1/2 cup sugar
1 tablespoon plus 2 teaspoons lemon juice
2 1/2 teaspoons ground ginger

Combine all the ingredients in a small saucepan. Stir constantly over medium heat, continuing for half a minute after the mixture begins to boil.

Raspberry-Avocado Cream

Makes about 1 cup

A striking color combination adds visual appeal, and the blend tastes delicious atop the Chocolate-Raspberry Cheesecakey Waffles (page 64) or the Dark Chocolate Cake Waffles (page 57).

> **1 ripe avocado (Hass or other variety)**
> **1/4 cup sugar**
> **2 teaspoons lemon juice**
> **1/2 teaspoon vanilla extract**
> **3/4 cup to 1 cup raspberries**

Scoop out the avocado. Place the avocado, sugar, lemon juice, and vanilla extract in a food processor and process until smooth and creamy. Place a few spoonfuls atop a waffle and embellish with raspberries.

If you don't have a food processor, mash the avocado in a medium bowl until all lumps are gone. Add the sugar, lemon juice, and vanilla extract, and mix until the sugar is dissolved.

Cinnamon Cream Cheese

Makes 1 cup

If you're craving cinnamon buns, spread some of this creamy delight onto the Original Cinnamon-Raisin Waffles (page 51) or the Yeast-Raised Cinnamon-Raisin Waffles (page 52).

1/4 cup raw cashew pieces
1 tablespoon lemon juice
1/4 cup maple syrup
6 ounces firm silken tofu, crumbled (about 2/3 cup)
1/2 teaspoon ground cinnamon
1/4 teaspoon salt

Place the cashew pieces, lemon juice, and maple syrup in a blender, and process for several minutes until the cashews are liquefied and the mixture is smooth and creamy. Stop as necessary to scrape down the sides of the blender bowl. Add the tofu, cinnamon, and salt, and blend until the mixture is smooth again.

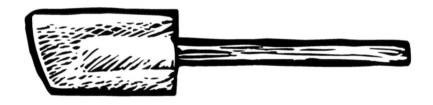

Creamy Maple-Chai Dream Sauce

Makes about 1 cup

The spicy warmth of this topping enhances the Sinful Cheesecakey Waffles (page 63) or the Dark Chocolate Cake Waffles (page 57).

> **6 ounces soft or firm silken tofu, crumbled (about 2/3 cup)**
> **1/3 cup maple syrup**
> **1/2 teaspoon vanilla extract**
> **1/4 teaspoon ground cinnamon**
> **1/4 teaspoon ground ginger**
> **1/8 teaspoon ground cardamom**
> **1/8 teaspoon ground clove**
> **1/8 teaspoon ground or grated nutmeg**

Place all ingredients in a blender and process until smooth and creamy. Stop as necessary to scrape down the sides of the blender bowl.

Note: For a "buttery" overtone, add 1/8 teaspoon of salt before blending.

Creamy Spiced Apple Pie Sauce

Makes 3/4 cup

This sweet and tart topping is much quicker to make than an apple pie, and is delicious hot or cold. For a taste reminiscent of a country dessert, spoon onto some Crunchy Steel City Waffles (page 48).

1/2 cup applesauce
1/4 cup vanilla soy yogurt
1 tablespoon vegan margarine
1 to 2 teaspoons sugar (optional)
1/4 teaspoon ground cinnamon
1/8 teaspoon allspice
1/8 teaspoon ground or grated nutmeg

Combine all the ingredients in a small saucepan. Stir constantly over medium heat just until the margarine is melted and the sugar is dissolved.

Simple Piña Colada-ish Topping

Makes about 1 cup

"Excuse me, does this beach have an outlet for a waffle iron?" This refreshing tropical treat goes nicely with the Kale-idoscopic Waffles (page 88), if you desire something adventurous.

3/4 cup pineapple, crushed or bits, with juice
1/4 cup plus 2 tablespoons coconut milk (not the "light" variety)
1 teaspoon sugar
1/2 teaspoon vanilla extract

Fill a measuring cup to the 3/4 cup mark with pineapple, adding pineapple juice to the cup so that all spaces between the pineapple are filled with juice up to the 3/4 cup mark. Combine all the ingredients in a small bowl and mix until the sugar is dissolved.

Amazing Amaretto Sauce

Makes about 3/4 cup

This simple but elegant syrup brings additional warmth and sweetness to the Almond-Amaranth Waffles (page 66) or the Sinful Cheesecakey Waffles (page 63).

> 1/4 cup amaretto liqueur (see note for alcohol-free version)
> 1/4 cup vegan margarine
> 1/4 cup plain or vanilla soy yogurt
> 1/4 cup sugar

Combine all the ingredients in a small saucepan. Stir constantly over medium heat just until the margarine is melted and the sugar is dissolved.

Note: For an alcohol-free version, omit liqueur and add 1/4 cup nondairy milk, 1 teaspoon almond extract, and 1 more tablespoon of sugar.

Carob Halvah Spread

Makes 1 cup

This thick and quick topping adds richness to a range of waffles. Put a bit on the Cashew-Carob-Molasses Waffles (page 67) for a supercharged carob experience.

> 1/2 cup agave nectar
> 1/2 cup tahini (sesame seed butter)
> 2 tablespoons roasted carob powder

Combine all the ingredients in a small bowl and mix until well blended. Serve at room temperature, warm slightly for a thinner consistency, or chill for a very thick consistency.

Cinnamon-Carob Halvah Spread: Add 1 1/2 teaspoons of ground cinnamon.

Mexican Chocolate Ice Cream

Makes 3 3/4 cups

The coolness of ice cream and warmth of cayenne create a smooth, palatable paradox. For a really richly spiced chocolate delight, spoon a few scoops between quarters of Chai Spice Waffles (page 65).

> 1 can (14 ounces) coconut milk (not the "light" variety)
> 1 1/4 cups soymilk or other nondairy milk
> 3/4 cup to 1 cup sugar
> 1/2 cup cocoa powder
> 3 tablespoons canola oil
> 2 teaspoons vanilla extract (see note)
> 1 1/4 teaspoons ground cinnamon
> 1/8 teaspoon ground cayenne
> 1/8 teaspoon salt
> 1/8 teaspoon xanthan gum powder (optional, to thicken slightly)

Combine all the ingredients in a blender and process for 2 to 3 minutes, or until the mixture is smooth and creamy. Stop midway to taste the mixture, and increase the sugar to the desired sweetness if necessary. Place the mixture in the freezer in a freezer-safe container for 45 to 60 minutes, or in the refrigerator for 90 minutes, to bring the temperature down.

Pour the mixture into an ice cream maker and freeze according to the manufacturer's directions. Enjoy immediately or place in the freezer for an hour for a harder consistency. If the ice cream has been in the freezer overnight or longer, allow it to soften at room temperature for 5 to 10 minutes before serving.

Note: Because alcohol may impede freezing, use alcohol-free extract if possible.

Mango-Vanilla Ice Cream

Makes 5 cups

This multiplies the mango factor of the Mango-Chili Waffles (page 69) or adds a tropical twist to the Sinful Cheesecakey Waffles (page 63).

> **2 ripe mangoes, chilled and finely chopped (about 2 cups, see note)**
> **3 cups soymilk or other nondairy milk**
> **3/4 cup to 1 cup sugar**
> **3 tablespoons canola oil**
> **1 tablespoon plus 1 teaspoon vanilla extract (see note)**
> **1/8 teaspoon xanthan gum powder (optional, to thicken slightly)**

Chop the mangoes and place them in the refrigerator to chill. Combine the soymilk, sugar, oil, vanilla extract, and xanthan gum powder in a blender and process for 2 to 3 minutes, or until the mixture is smooth and creamy. Stop midway to taste the mixture, and increase the sugar to the desired sweetness if necessary. Place the mixture in the freezer in a freezer-safe container for 45 to 60 minutes, or in the refrigerator for at least 90 minutes, to bring the temperature down.

Pour the mixture into an ice cream maker and freeze according to the manufacturer's directions. Fold in the chopped mangoes. Enjoy immediately or place in the freezer for an hour for a harder consistency. If the ice cream has been in the freezer overnight or longer, allow it to soften at room temperature for 5 to 10 minutes before serving.

Note: If you don't have fresh mangoes, you may substitute 2 cups of previously frozen, finely chopped mango.

Note: Because alcohol may impede freezing, use alcohol-free extract if possible.

Mango-Vanilla-Coconut Ice Cream: Add 1 can (14 ounces) of coconut milk and reduce the soymilk to 1 1/4 cups.

Basil-Orange Ice Cream

Makes 3 3/4 cups

This chilly confection is particularly refreshing for summertime waffles, especially if fresh basil is growing in the garden. For orange-basil abundance, pair with the Orange-Basil-Cornmeal Waffles (page 76).

> 1 can (14 ounces) coconut milk (not the "light" variety)
> 1 1/4 cups soymilk or other nondairy milk
> 3/4 cup to 1 cup sugar
> 1/2 cup packed fresh basil (lemon, lime, or sweet basil)
> 3 tablespoons canola oil
> 1 1/4 teaspoons orange extract (see note)
> 1 teaspoon vanilla extract (see note)
> 1/8 teaspoon xanthan gum powder (optional, to thicken slightly)

Combine all the ingredients in a blender and process for 2 to 3 minutes, or until the mixture is smooth and the basil leaves are very finely chopped. Stop midway to taste the mixture, and increase the sugar to the desired sweetness if necessary. Place the mixture in the freezer in a freezer-safe container for 45 to 60 minutes, or in the refrigerator for at least 90 minutes, to bring the temperature down.

Pour the mixture into an ice cream maker and freeze according to the manufacturer's directions. Enjoy immediately or place in the freezer for an hour for a harder consistency. If the ice cream has been in the freezer overnight or longer, allow it to soften at room temperature for 5 to 10 minutes before serving.

Note: Because alcohol may impede freezing, use alcohol-free extract if possible.

Flavory-Savory Waffle Toppings

Forget the myth that only sweet toppings may go on waffles. Whether you wish to add excitement to a neutral waffle or increase the moisture and flavor of an already-flavorful waffle, these toppings will liven up the party. As with the sweet toppings, experiment freely and try them on whichever waffles you wish. Influences include Thai (Coconut-Cashew-Basil Sauce, page 118), Mediterranean (Kalamata Olive and Sun-dried Tomato Hummus, page 128), Southern (Southern Fried Tofu and Waffles, page 126), and more. If you're feeling really bold, make a few different toppings and try them on different portions of the same waffle.

Savory Cashew-Mushroom Sauce

Makes 1 1/4 cups

Paired with the Umami Mama Waffles (page 81), this topping creates a richness that will satisfy cravings for pizza or other savory foods. It also meshes well with the Spanakowafflita (page 86).

- 2 cups baby portabella (brown crimini) mushrooms, thinly sliced
- 2 green onions, finely chopped
- 2 medium garlic cloves, crushed
- 2 tablespoons cashew butter, unsalted
- 2 tablespoons soy sauce
- 3 tablespoons water, divided
- 1/4 cup plain soy yogurt

Slice the mushrooms, chop the green onions, crush the garlic, and set aside. Heat the cashew butter, soy sauce, and 1 tablespoon of the water in a medium frying pan over medium heat, stirring and scraping the pan frequently with a spatula. Continue for 2 to 3 minutes, or until the cashew butter has softened and dissolved into the soy sauce.

Combine the mushrooms, green onions and garlic with the mixture in the pan. Sauté for another 4 to 6 minutes, turning frequently and adding 1 tablespoon of the remaining water every 2 minutes. Keep the mixture just moist enough to fry and brown slightly, so that it just begins to develop a crust. Stir in the soy yogurt and heat for another minute, scraping the pan frequently to avoid burning.

Coconut-Cashew-Basil Sauce

Makes about 1 cup

This creamy, moderately sweet, and slightly tangy sauce incorporates Thai influence and provides a twist to the Orange-Basil-Cornmeal Waffles (page 76).

> 3/4 cup coconut milk (not the "light" variety)
> 1/4 cup cashew butter, unsalted
> 2 tablespoons packed fresh basil (lime, lemon, or sweet basil)
> 2 teaspoons lime juice
> 1 tablespoon sugar
> 1/8 teaspoon salt

Combine all the ingredients in a blender and process for 30 to 60 seconds, or until smooth. If you don't have a blender, manually chop the basil leaves as finely as possible, and mix all the ingredients by hand until well blended.

Cilantro-Lime Tahini Sauce

Makes 3/4 cup

This variation from traditional tahini sauce, which often uses lemon juice and parsley, accents the Chili-Lime Felafel Waffles (page 85) nicely.

> 1/2 cup plain soy yogurt
> 1/4 cup tahini (sesame seed butter)
> 2 tablespoons lime juice
> 1 tablespoon finely chopped fresh cilantro (see note)
> 1/4 teaspoon salt

Combine all the ingredients in a small bowl, breaking up any clumps of tahini and mixing until well blended.

Note: You may substitute 1 tablespoon of finely chopped fresh parsley for the cilantro.

You Make Miso Tangy Dipping Sauce

Makes 3/4 cup

Melding Italian and Asian influences, this blend heightens the savoriness of waffles including the Caramelized Onion and Garlic Waffles (page 83) and the Umami Mama Waffles (page 81).

> 1/2 cup olive oil
> 1/4 cup balsamic vinegar
> 1 tablespoon light or chickpea miso
> 1 1/2 teaspoons sugar (or slightly more to taste)
> 1/8 teaspoon freshly ground black pepper
> dash of ground cayenne

Combine all the ingredients in a small bowl and stir with a whisk, breaking up any chunks of miso. Dip your favorite flavory-savory waffle into the mixture and enjoy.

Note: For added spiciness, add 2 teaspoons of dried basil and 1 teaspoon of dried oregano. Cover and place in the refrigerator for 2 hours prior to serving, allowing the flavors to blend.

Mint Raita

Makes 1 1/2 cups

Relatively simple so that the mint shines through, this sauce adds a refreshing accent to the Spicy Carrot-Raisin Waffles (page 75) or Some Awesome Samosa Waffles (page 95).

> 1 cup plain soy yogurt
> 1/2 medium cucumber, peeled, seeded, and finely diced (roughly 1 cup)
> 2 tablespoons packed fresh spearmint leaves, finely chopped
> 1 teaspoon sugar
> 1/4 teaspoon salt
> dash of ground cayenne (optional)

Combine all the ingredients in a small bowl and stir until well blended. Cover and place in the refrigerator for 2 hours prior to serving, allowing the flavors to blend.

Black Bean-Mango Tango

Makes 2 cups

This sweet, tangy, and refreshing blend dances well alongside the Mango-Chili Waffles (page 69) or the Refried Bean, Rice, and Cornmeal Waffles (page 79).

> 1 ripe mango, finely chopped (about 1 cup, see note)
> 1 can (15 ounces) black beans, rinsed
> 2 tablespoons lime juice
> 2 tablespoons olive oil
> 2 teaspoons finely chopped fresh cilantro (see note)
> 3/4 teaspoon chili powder
> 1/2 teaspoon paprika
> 1/4 teaspoon salt

Combine all the ingredients in a small bowl and stir until evenly mixed. Cover and place in the refrigerator for 1 to 2 hours, allowing the flavors to blend. Stir again just before serving.

Note: If you don't have a fresh mango, you may substitute 1 cup of previously frozen, finely chopped mango.

Note: If cilantro's not your thing, you can omit it or substitute 2 teaspoons of finely chopped fresh parsley.

Southwestern Beans & Greens

Makes 7 to 9 cups

This rich, chili-like dish works well as a substantive topping for larger parties or as a complete entrée for smaller gatherings. It goes especially well with the Yeast-Raised Cornmeal Chili-Dippin' Waffles (page 91). Leftovers can be frozen for future lunches.

> 1 1/2 pounds collard greens, chopped, fresh or frozen
> 2 cups onions, diced
> 1/2 cup baby portabella (brown crimini) mushrooms, finely chopped
> 2 medium cloves garlic, crushed
> 1/2 cup olive oil, divided (see note)
> 1 can (28 ounces) crushed tomatoes
> 1 can (15 ounces) diced tomatoes
> 2 cans (15 ounces each) black beans, rinsed and drained
> 1 can (15 ounces) pinto beans, rinsed and drained
> 1/2 cup nutritional yeast flakes
> 2 tablespoons dried basil
> 2 tablespoons chili powder
> 2 tablespoons ground cumin
> 2 tablespoons molasses (blackstrap or other variety)
> 2 tablespoons sugar
> 3/4 to 1 1/2 teaspoons salt
> 1/2 teaspoon liquid smoke (optional)
> 1/4 teaspoon freshly ground black pepper
> 1/8 teaspoon ground cayenne

Chop the collard greens into bite-sized pieces, dice the onions, chop the mushrooms, and set aside. Combine the onion, garlic, and 2 tablespoons of the oil in a large non-aluminum saucepan. Sauté over medium heat for 5 minutes or until slightly browned, stirring every 1 or 2 minutes to avoid burning. Add the mushroom and sauté for another 3 minutes. Add the remaining 1/4 cup plus 2 tablespoons of oil, crushed tomatoes, diced tomatoes, black beans, pinto beans, nutritional yeast, basil, chili powder, cumin, sugar, salt, liquid smoke, black pepper, and cayenne, and stir well. When the mixture starts to boil, add the collards to the pot and stir them into the mixture. They will greatly decrease in volume as they heat. Reduce the heat to low. Simmer covered for 45 minutes, stirring every 5 to 10 minutes to prevent burning. To give the flavors more time to blend, let stand in the fridge overnight.

Note: You may reduce the total amount of oil to 1/4 cup if you wish.

Spicy Sloppy Tofu & Portabella

Makes 4 1/2 cups

Suitable for a main dish, this is essentially a deluxe vegan sloppy Joe. Spoon a generous serving of this satisfyingly savory topping between 2 quarters of Yeast-Raised Waffles (page 42) to form a sloppy tofu wafflewich.

14 ounces extra-firm tofu, prepared in advance (see How-To, page 125)
1 cup finely chopped baby portabella (brown crimini) mushrooms
3/4 cup finely chopped red onion
1/2 cup finely chopped green pepper
2 medium cloves garlic, crushed
1/4 cup plus 2 tablespoons olive oil, divided
1 can (28 ounces) crushed tomatoes
1/3 cup molasses (blackstrap or other variety)
1/3 cup nutritional yeast flakes
1/4 cup finely chopped sun-dried tomatoes, preserved in olive oil or rehydrated (optional)
2 tablespoons brown sugar
1 tablespoon dried basil
1 tablespoon chili powder
1 tablespoon cider vinegar
1 to 1 1/2 teaspoons salt
1 teaspoon dried mustard powder
1 teaspoon dried oregano
1/4 to 1/2 teaspoon liquid smoke (optional)
1/4 teaspoon freshly ground black pepper
1/8 to 1/4 teaspoon ground cayenne

After the tofu has been prepared, crumble it into small pieces, and set aside in a small bowl. Chop the mushrooms, onion, and green pepper, and set aside.

Combine the onion, garlic, and 2 tablespoons of the oil in a large non-aluminum saucepan. Sauté over medium heat for 5 minutes or until slightly browned, stirring every minute to avoid burning. Add 2 more tablespoons of oil, the mushrooms, and green pepper, and sauté for 5 more minutes. Reduce the heat to low, and add the remaining 2 tablespoons of oil, crushed tomatoes, molasses, nutritional yeast, sun-dried tomatoes, brown sugar, basil, chili powder, vinegar, salt, mustard powder, oregano, liquid smoke, black pepper, and cayenne. Stir until well blended.

Pour the prepared tofu into the mixture. Warm the entire mixture over medium heat, stirring every 1 to 2 minutes, just until it begins to boil. Reduce the heat to low. Simmer uncovered for 45 minutes, stirring every 5 to 10 minutes to prevent burning.

How-To: Prepare Freeze and Squeeze Tofu

Open and drain the block of tofu at least 1 day in advance, and cut widthwise into 8 slices, each roughly 1 inch thick. Seal them in a freezer-tight bag or container and place it in the freezer overnight. Then remove from the freezer and thaw. Placing the bag or container in a pot of hot water can speed the thawing process to under an hour. Press 1 or 2 thawed slices at a time between your palms, squeezing out as much of the water as you can. It should now have a spongier texture that will enable it to absorb more flavor.

Southern Fried Tofu & Waffles

Makes 2 1/3 cups

Based upon the popular non-vegan southern dish of fried chicken and waffles, this spicy topping plays well with the Yeast-Raised Cornmeal Chili-Dippin' Waffles (page 91) or the Tropically Tanned Naked Waffles (page 38). Drizzle with a combination of your favorite hot sauce and melted vegan margarine.

> 14 ounces extra-firm tofu, prepared in advance (see How-To, page 125)
> 1/4 cup all-purpose flour or gluten-free flour of choice
> 1/4 cup cornmeal
> 1/4 cup nutritional yeast flakes
> 1 tablespoon sugar
> 1 1/2 teaspoons ground cumin
> 1 1/2 teaspoons salt
> 1 1/4 teaspoons garlic powder
> 1 1/4 teaspoons onion powder
> 1/2 teaspoon freshly ground black pepper
> 1/8 to 1/4 teaspoon ground cayenne
> 3/4 cup soymilk or other nondairy milk
> 1 tablespoon plus 2 teaspoons cornstarch
> 1/4 cup canola oil, divided

After the tofu has been prepared, chop each slice into cubes roughly an inch wide, and set aside.

Combine the flour, cornmeal, nutritional yeast, sugar, cumin, salt, garlic powder, onion powder, black pepper, and cayenne in a large, shallow dish and stir with a whisk. Combine the soymilk and cornstarch in a medium bowl and stir with a whisk until the cornstarch is mostly dissolved.

Heat 2 tablespoons of the oil over medium to high heat in a large frying pan, until a small test drop of the soymilk and cornstarch mixture sizzles upon contact. Using your hands or a spoon, briefly dip several tofu cubes at a time into the soymilk and cornstarch mixture, roll them in the flour mixture, and place in the pan. Fry the battered tofu cubes for 5 to 7 minutes, adding the remaining 2 tablespoons of oil if the pan becomes dry, and turning the cubes as each side becomes slightly browned.

Note: For additional flavor, drizzle 1 to 2 tablespoons of the remaining soymilk mixture onto the cooking tofu cubes, and then sprinkle 1 to 2 tablespoons of the remaining flour mixture onto the cubes, just before turning them a second time.

Kalamata Olive & Sun-dried Tomato Hummus

Makes 3 1/2 cups

Blending umami with tartness, spice, and texture, this topping walks hand-in-hand with the Caramelized Onion and Garlic Waffles (page 83) or the Naked Vegan Waffles (page 37).

> 2 cans (15 ounces each) chickpeas, rinsed and drained
> 1/3 cup water
> 1/4 cup lemon juice
> 1/4 cup olive oil
> 1/4 cup tahini (sesame seed butter)
> 2 tablespoons nutritional yeast flakes
> 2 medium cloves garlic
> 3/4 teaspoon salt
> 1/2 teaspoon chili powder
> 1/2 teaspoon paprika
> 1/16 to 1/8 teaspoon ground cayenne
> 1/4 cup pitted Kalamata olives
> 1/4 cup sun-dried tomatoes, preserved in olive oil or rehydrated

Process the chickpeas, water, lemon juice, oil, tahini, nutritional yeast, garlic, salt, chili powder, paprika, and cayenne in a food processor until smooth. Add the olives and sun-dried tomatoes, and pulse for 2 to 3 seconds at a time until pieces are the desired size.

If you don't have a food processor, mash the chickpeas, crush the garlic, and chop the olives and sun-dried tomatoes by hand. Then mix all ingredients in a medium bowl until well blended.

Note: For an added twist, top the hummus with a swirl of the reddish-hued olive oil from the sun-dried tomatoes, alongside a few dashes of paprika and a fresh lemon wedge.

Ideas for Ultra-Quick Toppings

Is your time extremely limited, or are you preparing for a very large event? Consider some of these vegan waffle toppings:

❖ any type of nut butter (e.g., peanut, almond, cashew), purchased pre-made or created at home with a food processor

❖ fresh, frozen, dried, or canned fruit, including pineapple or berries

❖ jam or preserves

❖ dried coconut

❖ soy yogurt (can be mixed with fruit)

❖ granola

❖ vegan cream cheese

❖ non-dairy ice cream

❖ vegan whipped toppings

❖ liquid sweeteners such as agave nectar and rice syrup

❖ store-bought hummus

❖ pre-made vegan chili

❖ guacamole or salsa

❖ beans with herbs and spices added—for example, chickpeas in a pre-made Indian spice blend, or vegan refried beans with cumin and cilantro

❖ vegan chocolate chips (may be melted to make a sauce)

❖ rice with spices, or incorporated into a pre-made vegan cooking sauce

❖ spicy tempeh

129

Organizing & Hosting a Waffle Party

Once you have purchased a waffle iron and enjoyed a few recipes on your own, you may be eager to share delicious food with others. Vegan waffle parties can be an excellent way to connect with others, while acknowledging that reduction and elimination of animal product consumption are keys to friendlier, healthier, and more sustainable living.

Here I share several important things we've learned over the years, in hopes that your waffle parties are wildly successful right from the start. If you've already thrown many food-related parties, some of the following material will be old hat for you. However, waffles do require some special considerations because they're prepared on the spot, and there are important things to keep in mind if you're reaching out to both vegan and non-vegan guests.

What is a Waffle Party?

A waffle party is a festive and stomach-filling social event where waffles are served, preferably hot off the iron, with delicious toppings. It can be a relatively simple gathering with just a few friends, or it can be an extravagant production with dozens of guests. The only major items needed are a waffle maker, a vegan waffle recipe, waffle making ingredients, and some hungry friends who are willing to bring vegan waffle toppings and have fun.

Why an Event Featuring Vegan Waffles?

The vegan waffle is especially well-suited for building awareness and increasing interconnectedness. Here are some of the most important reasons to host and enjoy a vegan waffle party:

❖ Even with excellent resources on delicious vegan cupcakes, cookies, and other vegan foods, there's still a great need to build awareness that baked goods can be done without dairy and eggs.

❖ Waffles are broadly recognized and enjoyed, and vegan ones often taste even better. Many people are especially surprised to learn that waffles can be vegan—then they wonder, "If waffles, why not other baked goods?"

❖ Waffles are fun, delicious, and versatile—they can function as a main course for breakfast, brunch, lunch, or dinner, or they can serve as a novel dessert.

❖ Waffles are inexpensive and relatively easy to make. Creating a batch of batter is simpler than preparing a complex 2- or 3-dish meal.

❖ Asking guests to bring vegan waffle toppings gives them an easy way to participate and share. For non-vegan friends, concocting a topping can be less intimidating than making a full vegan dish.

❖ Those just learning the benefits of a plant-based diet and lifestyle may feel a bit overwhelmed at first. Most of us have been there ourselves. Vegan waffle parties offer a fun and gentle way to enjoy food while altering common misconceptions. For example, an array of toppings illustrates that there really are many plant-based food options available.

History of the Waffle Party

For decades, one of the world's most fascinating foods was viewed merely as a breakfast item. In 1998, this misconception ended. In our small apartment in Baltimore, Maryland, creative forces converged to catalyze what is now believed to be the world's longest-running annual waffle party.

Each year, guests and hosts have continued to expand the boundaries of waffle topping possibilities, going far beyond traditional maple syrup. They have discovered that waffles can harmonize with ingredients including spices, veggies, curries, and tofu. Creative guests bring toppings they have always desired to try on a waffle. In the company of other gastronomic pioneers, they freely experiment and achieve new levels of culinary excitement.

In 2001, we moved to Pittsburgh, Pennsylvania, continuing the tradition there. In November of that year, responding to a question on the word "waffle," The Word Detective (word-detective.com) noted that the earliest known mention of the word in English (1744) includes a "waffle frolic." This was apparently an event centered around making and eating waffles. It is possible that similar events could have occurred even earlier in other parts of the world. Upon discovering this a few years later, we were excited to realize that we may have revived an almost-forgotten festivity.

As we gained awareness of the impacts of our diets and lifestyles, the waffle party became vegetarian and then vegan. In May 2008, several cities participated in the first Global Vegan Waffle Party. Some websites even declared a new holiday: World Vegan Waffle Day, the Saturday right before the last Monday in May.

With your participation, the positive energy and awareness will continue to expand. More and more people across the globe will recognize that delicious baked goods do not require eggs or dairy.

Developing a Vision

In *The Seven Habits of Highly Effective People*, Stephen Covey advises, "Begin with the end in mind." Such a mindset helps to ensure that you create the event you really want. There are many possible ways to throw a waffle party, and many reasons for throwing one. Here are a few questions to ask yourself as you begin to plan:

❖ For what reasons do you wish to throw a waffle party? In other words, what is the primary purpose of the event? Some possible reasons include: just for fun, getting to know new people, introducing others to vegetarianism and veganism, impressing friends with your creativity and cooking acumen, or getting to know other vegetarians and vegans in your community.

❖ Who is your audience and how large is the event going to be? Both of these may be driven by the answer to the first question regarding purpose. These answers may also depend upon the resources you have available, including space, time, equipment, and money.

❖ How long would you like the party to last? You might decide to have an open house for several hours, or you might wish to limit your event to 2 or 3 hours.

❖ How much time would you like to spend visiting with guests? If you're having a large party, the waffle baking alone may take significant time and effort.

The answers to these questions will help you to organize the event in a way that generates the desired results. For example, if a primary purpose is to get to know new people, and you want to have at least 2 hours to chat with guests, you'll probably want to minimize the time you spend baking waffles in the kitchen during the party. On the other hand, if your primary purpose is to show off how delicious vegan food can be, and to introduce others to delicious vegan food, then you may end up spending much more time baking—but you'll still enjoy it because it fits your purpose for throwing the party.

As you develop your vision, remember that it needs to be fun for you as well as your guests. If you feel like you're making the party bigger or more complex than you can handle, consider simplifying it or asking for more help. If you're not having fun, your guests will sense it and they won't have a good time either. And that pretty much defeats the purpose of having a party.

After several years of throwing annual waffle parties, Jen and I reworked our vision because we weren't satisfied with some aspects of previous events. We enjoyed the excitement and variety of a large crowd, and I really enjoyed baking the waffles, but we also wanted more time to visit with guests. Most people would show up during the first hour or two, during which time I was quite busy baking waffles. By the time I finished, most of the guests had already been there a few hours and had begun to leave. This gave me little time to visit.

Clarifying our vision for the party led us to some innovative solutions. Using an online event planning and invitation site, I designated 2 arrival times spaced 2 hours apart (6:00 PM and 8:00 PM), with each "shift" allowing around 20 people. I spent just under an hour making fresh waffles at each of those times. In between, I turned off the irons and took time to mingle with guests, sample toppings, and enjoy other aspects of the party. This provided a better balance for us.

As you define what you want, consider developing a title or theme for your party. If you're artistically inclined, you can even create a logo or theme song! For example, one of our parties was entitled "Vegan, Green and Delicious" because we wanted to emphasize the environmental benefits of a vegan lifestyle. We also took other steps to make the party more ecologically friendly. If you really enjoy chocolate, you might host a party where guests bring vegan waffle toppings containing cocoa. If you like spicy foods, your gathering might feature an array of southern Indian toppings. The possibilities are literally endless.

Food Preparation Tips

For many types of parties, all of the food can be prepared in advance. Waffles, however, are best served hot out of the iron. Baking a fresh vegan waffle for each guest is part of what makes a waffle party special. This requires a few logistical considerations. You can take steps to minimize the amount of time guests must wait for food, increase the speed with which you create waffles, or both.

Test drive the recipes in advance

To reiterate a key point, always try the recipes you plan to use in advance, even if it means halving each recipe so you can bake 1 or 2 test waffles. If time allows, bake a test waffle on each iron you plan to use. This will lessen the odds of a waffler's worst nightmare: a severe sticking or charring incident. You can freeze any surplus test waffles for later consumption.

Prepare wet & dry batter portions beforehand

It can be difficult to focus on details like measuring ingredients during the party, while you're also hosting and talking to guests. To increase baking efficiency and maintain sanity during your event, measure out the wet and dry batter portions in advance. If you're making more than one kind of waffle, label each jar or container of wet ingredients and its corresponding bowl of dry ingredients so you know which portion goes with which. If you do this the night before the party, keep the wet mixture portion in a sealed container in the refrigerator and the dry mixture portion in a covered bowl on the counter.

Yeast-raised and flaxseed-containing recipes will have 3 separate portions. Yeast-raised recipes will include the following: the yeast-raised portion that is left to rise for several hours, the additional liquid ingredients added shortly before baking, and the baking soda or baking powder that is dissolved in the liquid just before adding the liquid to the yeast-raised portion.

For flaxseed-containing recipes, keep the flaxseed separate until mixing all the portions together. Its binding power and thickness can increase when sitting in liquid for extended periods, which may increase the odds of waffles sticking to the iron. Adding more water afterwards may resolve this, but not always.

An hour before baking, take the premixed wet portion out of the refrigerator so it has time to warm slightly. Then, within 15 minutes of baking, mix together the portions according to the recipe's directions.

To maximize waffle-making efficiency while minimizing waffle batter waste, consider preparing batches that will make roughly 8 waffles each. This generally means doubling a recipe. Smaller batches result in more frequent mixing during the party, and larger batches may result in more mixed but unused batter at the end. If you're hosting a large party and don't want to do all the advance batter preparation on your own, consider hosting a small "batter prep party" with a few friends or roommates the night before the event.

The following photos illustrate premixed wet and dry ingredients for several batches of vegan waffles. The small labels have abbreviations indicating each type of waffle, to ensure proper matching of wet and dry portions. Note the reuse of beverage and food containers.

Premixed wet ingredients for several batches of waffles

Premixed dry ingredients for several batches of waffles

Secure a second iron

Another way to increase cooking capacity is to borrow or purchase a second waffle iron. Suppose a single iron bakes a waffle large enough for 1 person in 4 minutes, and it takes an additional 2 minutes to remove a waffle from the iron, allow the iron to fully reheat, and pour batter for the next waffle. Excluding any time needed to prepare fresh batches of batter, your maximum capacity will be around 10 waffles per hour. If you're inviting a large number of people, this may not be acceptable. Because we host large parties each year, we own several irons and I usually run 3 at once. Just note that running multiple irons takes some practice, and it requires a system for keeping track of multiple cooking times.

Cut waffles into quarters

If obtaining more irons is not an option, but you're still concerned about guest wait time, you can encourage a slower waffle consumption rate. Simply divide each fresh waffle into quarters with a pizza cutter. This allows several guests to start eating at once, instead of one guest getting a whole waffle while everyone else continues to wait. By the time guests finish topping their waffle quarters and eating them, another batch is ready. This approach also makes it easier to try different toppings without mixing incompatible ones, e.g., savory toppings on one quarter, and sweet toppings on the next.

Have a two-shift event

Yet another possibility, mentioned earlier, is to decrease the speed at which your guests arrive by offering more than one arrival time, with an attendance cap placed on each (see "Developing a Vision," page 133). This will avoid a large rush of hungry guests all at once, and will give you space to breathe and mingle between arrival times.

Host a DIY waffle baking adventure

If you want to decrease the time you spend baking during the party, you can allow guests the opportunity to make their own waffles. However, this is wise only if your kitchen is large enough to handle the additional traffic, and only if you have at least one extra backup iron in case of a sticking incident. Your guests will not know the nuances of your particular iron, and a single failure to spray oil on the grids can create a mess and an extended wait.

Create an emergency backup if needed

If you realize that you're going to have more attendees than you can manage with your cooking capacity, and none of the above strategies will do the trick, there is a last resort: serving reheated frozen waffles alongside your fresh homemade waffles. In my opinion, frozen vegan waffles will never quite stack up to freshly baked ones, but some are still pretty tasty—especially with toppings. Just heat up a few store-bought waffles in the toaster while you're also baking fresh waffles. Depending on your schedule, you could also bake a few batches of homemade "backup waffles" the night before, put them in the freezer, and reheat them as needed during the party. See more on storing and reheating waffles on page 19.

Vegan Party Etiquette

When you're inviting people with a range of eating preferences and asking them to bring food, you can avoid several potential pitfalls.

Catering to a mix of lifestyles

Throwing parties for a combination of vegan and non-vegan individuals can be great fun, as it encourages togetherness and allows many people to try something different. However, there are a few things to keep in mind.

First, provide guests with advance notice regarding the guidelines for ingredients, and be as clear as possible. This will help to prevent embarrassing and uncomfortable situations. Be prepared for the possibility that some guests may still overlook the guidelines, especially if they're already inundated with email and have a busy schedule.

If one of your guests brings a non-vegan item, you face the balancing act of making them feel as welcome as possible while maintaining a comfortable environment for your vegan guests. You might start by thanking them for bringing a dish, letting them know they made an honest oversight, and explaining the need to maintain a comfortable and safe environment for all of your guests. Then you might discreetly offer to store their topping in the refrigerator for them until they're ready to go home, or place it on a side table with a label very clearly indicating its non-vegan ingredients. It's up to you.

The first year our waffle party was vegetarian, a friend who had attended in previous years overlooked this change and accidentally brought a flesh-based dish. He was obviously embarrassed, but we still thanked him for bringing it, placed it on one of the side tables for guests who weren't vegetarian, and made sure it was clearly labeled. Nowadays, we might do something similar with the occasional egg- or dairy-containing dish, but would likely place a flesh-containing dish entirely out of sight.

Secondly, clearly inform your vegan guests if you are also having non-vegan guests, and vice-versa. This lets your vegan guests know to be on the lookout for non-vegan items brought by accident. While as a host you should do your best to check for such items, it can be difficult to spot everything.

Thirdly, in your invitation materials, you may wish to emphasize that while all the food will be vegan, everyone is welcome regardless of their current eating habits. Our invitations always state, "You don't have to be vegan, but the topping you bring does." This helps to set an inclusive tone and implies that guests will be expected to embrace the same attitude.

Being mindful of other dietary requirements

When planning your party, you'll need to decide how many types of requirements you can comfortably accommodate, so that you can announce them up front. For example, are you planning to provide gluten-free waffles, soy-free waffles and toppings, or even a raw vegan alternative to waffles? Will some or all of your items also be organic? It's entirely up to you how inclusive you wish to be. If a few of your guests have allergies to common ingredients that aren't in the waffles, but that may be in some of the toppings, you can ask guests to label toppings with their name, the dish name, and the ingredients. This way, anyone who must avoid specific items can see what's in each dish, and can track down the chef with any questions.

Making it easy for guests to get to know one another

Name tags sound like a no-brainer, but I don't see them at many parties, and we often forget them at ours. This is especially important if you've invited guests from your regular "vegan food outing group" as well as guests from other settings. Encouraging everyone to add something creative to their name tag, such as their favorite flavor, can serve as an ice breaker.

Welcoming both positive & constructive feedback

When hosting an event with a social consciousness theme, you'll naturally attract some guests who set high standards for themselves and for others. Some may consider it their ethical duty to inform you of things that could be improved. Even when you've done your best, they will find something you've overlooked—perhaps you could have avoided a few paper plates, or perhaps you could have made sure all the drinks were organic. Maybe you could have asked your non-vegan neighbor not to wear a leather outfit to the event.

The best I can suggest is to be prepared for such things, and recognize that you will never make everyone 100% happy. Nonetheless, you may profoundly impact some of your guests, save many lives, provide inspiration, and create more change than you realize. This can be difficult to measure, but it will likely dwarf any seemingly negative energy you happen to receive.

Remind yourself of your primary purpose for hosting the event. For example, is it to create a certain appearance of yourself, or is it to have fun while improving the world? With that in mind, embrace constructive feedback that may help you to fulfill your purpose even better next time. On the other hand, discard feedback that doesn't help to you achieve your purpose.

At the same time, don't get so caught up in hosting a perfect event that you overlook all the little compliments you receive. Because hosting often involves spotting and fixing anything that may be wrong or out of place, it can be easy to focus on what's going wrong and lose track of what's going right. Focus on the parts that seem to be the most fun for everyone, and ask yourself how you can create even more of that next time.

Physical Setting Logistics

The unique nature of the waffle party also demands some special considerations regarding physical layout. Following are ideas for maintaining a comfortable atmosphere for everyone.

Entryway

If you're going to be cooking waffles in the kitchen as guests are still arriving, you won't be available to answer the door, hang coats, and so on. Thus, you can use signs to direct people where to put their shoes and coats, or you might ask a friend to help answer the door during the initial rush.

Dining room

Visualize yourself as a hungry and thirsty guest who has just arrived. Take a few moments to mentally run through the actions you would take. For example, what do you look for as you prepare to eat and drink, and in what order? Prior to grabbing a waffle, you'll probably look for a plate and a fork, and possibly a napkin. Hopefully these items will be conveniently nearby, and won't require pushing through a crowd or standing in line again. After grabbing a waffle, you'll be seeking toppings, and then possibly something to drink. You can do this "pretend you're a guest" visualization as you're planning, and again the day of the party as you're getting everything set up.

One dining room item in particular will save you significant effort if you plan to have a large crowd. Place the freshly baked waffle set-out and pick-up point as close to the waffle irons as you possibly can. This way you don't have to squeeze through a crowded room to put the fresh waffles on the table.

Kitchen

If you have a small kitchen or are expecting enough guests to require running multiple waffle irons, you may need to take additional steps to ensure that your kitchen remains an efficient and safe working space.

Do whatever you can to minimize kitchen traffic. Otherwise, guests will be walking through as you're baking waffles, posing a potential safety hazard. Keep as many of your food and drink supplies as possible in other rooms. Utilize coolers for drinks and ice so that guests don't need to visit the refrigerator. You don't want anyone, including yourself, getting a burn or having a large bowl of batter spilled on them. If you have a very small kitchen with a back door, you may wish to place a sign outside directing people to the front door.

Because waffle irons are high-wattage appliances, determine the limits of your house or apartment's electrical system before running multiple irons at once. One year we faced the embarrassment of having the lights and stereo go out during our party, when I attempted to turn on the microwave while waffle irons were running. Apparently I had plugged too many items into the same circuit. After I switched one of them to a different outlet, all was fine. In kitchens with older wiring, running too many high-wattage items might even present a safety hazard.

If your party is in the summer, you may wish to place a fan in a kitchen window to exhaust heat, moisture, and the smoke that the hot cooking oil can sometimes produce. This is especially important if you're using a few waffle irons at once. If it's during colder weather, have a fan readily available near a window or door that's easy to open if necessary.

Keeping It Environmentally Friendly

Introducing others to creative vegan food can benefit the environment by reducing animal-based agriculture. However, you don't want to cancel out any positive impacts by generating a lot of waste. This is particularly likely when you're having a large party, because the idea of having a pile of dishes to wash can make the immediate convenience of disposables especially tempting. Below are a few tips for minimizing any negative ecological impacts of your party. Keep in mind that you'll also be setting a good example for others.

❖ Turn off waffle irons when not used for extended periods.

❖ If you don't have enough plates, cups, utensils, or cloth napkins, borrow some from a neighbor or friend, or consider having guests bring some of their own items.

❖ If you host large parties frequently, consider reusable, dishwasher-safe plates, cups, and utensils made of recycled plastic. Just like disposable dinnerware, it is lightweight, non-breakable, and stackable in a minimal amount of space. By placing out several small bins for dirty plates, cups, and utensils, along with signs asking guests to scrape food into the trashcan before stacking their plates, you can reduce your cleanup efforts to loading and unloading the dishwasher a few times. We've done this for two of our waffle parties, and have been very pleased with the results.

❖ Because waffles with toppings can be messy, completely avoiding paper towels or napkins may be difficult at a larger party. In most cases, however, it doesn't take an entire paper towel or napkin to absorb a small amount of food from one's face or hands. Prior to the party, tear paper towels or paper napkins into halves or quarters. Someone can always grab a few more if they really need to.

Other Fun Ideas

Do you wish to provide an exceptionally creative experience for your guests? Here are some additional ways to make your vegan waffle party even more memorable and successful. Global Vegan Waffle Party hosts in other cities have already raised the bar by introducing some of these ideas:

❖ Bake waffles in conjunction with a bake sale for your favorite cause. If you have limited space where you live, ask to utilize a community organization's kitchen and dining area, or partner with a local business in a mutually beneficial way that helps them to draw customers.

❖ Host a vegan waffle party as a friendlier alternative to a regular non-vegan event that occurs in your area, e.g., a fish fry or non-vegan pancake breakfast.

❖ Suggest a vegan waffle party as an event for an existing local vegan or vegetarian group.

❖ Ask guests to share candidly what they liked most or least about the party, using an anonymous note card box.

❖ Encourage guests to vote on their favorite waffle topping, and offer a prize to the winning chef.

❖ Convince your friends to host other vegan food events on adjacent weekends, creating an entire month of vegan-themed food parties.

❖ Ask local businesses if they would like to sponsor your event, making a contribution in return for ads placed on your event's web page or on materials displayed at your event. You can donate proceeds to a worthy cause.

❖ Offer other types of activities at your waffle party. This might include live entertainment, an educational film, or vegan food-making demonstrations.

❖ Use your imagination!

Inaugural Global Vegan Waffle Party Hosts & Cities

The below individuals and groups have helped to get the party started in its first few years, building the initial momentum. There's still tremendous room for spreading awareness. Your participation can help to move it forward!

- Aletha at New World Dawn, Pontiac, MI, US
- Alexis and Waffle Frolic, Ithaca, NY, US
- Alisa F. at Go Dairy Free, Las Vegas, NV, US
- Allie C. and the Rogue Brunch Brigade, Baltimore, MD, US
- Amanda L. and the San Francisco Vegan Desserts Meetup, CA, US
- Amber M. and Café Green, Washington, DC, US
- Autumn at Living Vegetarian, Old Fort, NC, US
- Avril S., South Wales, UK
- Betsy S. at Beer is Vegan, Durham, NC, US
- Billie D. at Wild Pure Heart, Braidwood, NSW, Australia
- Blakely S., Boston, MA, US
- Brianne, Halifax, NS, Canada
- Bridget C., Canberra, ACT, Australia
- C. "Peanut" Vardaros, Everberg, Belgium
- Café Evolution, Florence, MA, US
- Chelsi H., Jessup, PA, US
- Clark at Raven Facts, Berkeley, CA, US
- Cynthia and students at Cal Poly Pomona, US
- Dallas at the Animal Rights Coalition, Minneapolis, MN, US
- Dave and Jen W., Pittsburgh, PA, US
- Dawn at Dawn's Custom Cakes, Cambridge, ON, Canada
- Dawn *et al.* at Waffle Shop, Pittsburgh, PA, US
- Derek and The Vegan Bus, Northampton, MA, US
- Dylan Y., Norman, OK, US
- Earl B. and the Tokyo Vegan Meetup, Japan
- Edy H. at Vegan Recipes from the Heart, Aptos, CA, US
- Elaine V. and Vegas Veg* Meetup, Las Vegas, NV, US
- Elizabeth R., Grand Rapids, MI, US
- Emily at creATE, Ann Arbor, MI, US
- Emily G., Cambridge, MA, US
- Emma W., Cockeysville, MD, US
- Ena H., Munich, Bavaria, Germany
- Fair Grounds Coffeehouse, Iowa City, IA, US
- Feather at Vegan Around the World, Los Angeles, CA, US
- Freya Dinshah at the American Vegan Society, Malaga, NJ, US
- Garrett W. at Gee, Think, Plainfield, NJ, US
- Gary L. at Compassion4Animals, Falls Church, VA, US
- Haroula G., Athens, Greece
- Heather D., Leah F., and the Fort Wayne Vegan/Vegetarians Group, IN, US
- Hollan H., Koloa, HI, US
- House of Pain Vegan Waffles, Montreal, QC, Canada

❖ Ida H., Noah L., VegOut NYC, and The Vegan Ideal, NY, US

❖ Jeanine H. and Delicious Donations, Braddock, PA, US

❖ Jeannie and the Chico Vegan Meetup, CA, US

❖ Jen at Devious Soybeans, Berkeley, CA, US

❖ Jennifer M. and Positively Veg*n Meetup, Fort Lauderdale, FL, US

❖ Jess at Cruelty Free WA, Fremantle, Western Australia

❖ Jessica C., Pendleton, SC, US

❖ Jessie Joy S., Boston, MA, US

❖ Judith at Big Raw and Vegan Blog, Klamath Falls, OR, US

❖ Kassi W., Bryan, TX, US

❖ Kathryn B., Los Angeles, CA, US

❖ Kerry S-D and Vegans of the Earth, Fort Ashby, WV, US

❖ Kim M., Sebastopol, CA, US

❖ Krystal Leigh A., Toledo, OH, US

❖ Lily K., Las Vegas, NV, US

❖ Lolo R. at Sweat Records, Miami, FL, US

❖ Lori Anne A., Raw Passion Bistro, and the Dayton Vegan Challenge, OH, US

❖ Lou's Vegan Pancake Wedding Breakfast, Charleston, SC, US

❖ M.E. Matthews, Boston, MA, US

❖ Malek K., Korat (Nakhon Ratchasima), Thailand

❖ Margaret I., Cambridge, MA, US

❖ Maria and Counter Culture Collective, Santa Cruz, CA, US

❖ Mary at Well on Wheels, Hamden, CT, US

❖ Meggie W. and Animal Allies Club, Orem, UT, US

❖ Melanie and John at The Wild Cow, Nashville, TN, US

❖ Meredith H., Vienna, VA, US

❖ Merri, Grosse Pointe, MI, US

❖ Michael S., Ithaca, NY, US

❖ Michelle R., Fullerton, CA, US

❖ Mike R., Guelph, ON, Canada

❖ Mimi T., Berkeley, CA, US

❖ Mommy and Me Brunch at Belly Sprout, Fullerton, CA, US

❖ Oh, Yeah! Ice Cream and Waffles, Pittsburgh, PA, US

❖ The Organic Sage, Hollywood, FL, US

❖ Rachel at Thistle and Yellow Rose, Edinburgh, Scotland

❖ Rachel C., New Britain, CT, US

❖ Rachel H., Spring Hill, FL, US

❖ Raelene C., Richmond, CA, US

❖ Rhett A., Jacksonville, FL, US

❖ Sinéad S., Vancouver, BC, Canada

❖ A Smexy Housewife, Harrisburg, PA, US

❖ Steven and Emerging Green Queers, Madison, WI, US

❖ Stevie's Waffle Wednesday, Tempe, AZ, US

❖ Supercarrot at Vegan Review Podcast, Philadelphia, PA, US

❖ Susie "Bumblebee," Carrboro, NC, US

❖ Toontz at Okara Mountain, Wisconsin, US

❖ Valerie S., Maitland, FL, US

❖ Wes A. and Vegans Rock Austin, TX, US

❖ Yvonne W., Wasaga Beach, ON, Canada

Glossary of Waffle Vernacular

If you plan to venture seriously into the realm of vegan waffles, it's important to know the lingo. Don't get caught being square at a round waffle party—or at any other waffle party, for that matter.

get yer grid on: Behave in a manner so indisputably cool that everyone wants to be around you, e.g., when you're baking delicious vegan waffles.

Global Vegan Waffle Party: An annual event that utilizes vegan waffles, toppings, and house parties to promote awareness about vegan food and lifestyles.

off the grid: Term used to describe a very successful and exciting waffle party.

Vaffeldagen: Waffle Day in Sweden, March 25.

vaffeldander: The small, crispy, burnt chips resulting from a waffle sticking to the iron badly.

Waffle Iron City: Pittsburgh, Pennsylvania has often been called "The Iron City" or "The Steel City" due to its industrial heritage. After waffle parties came to Pittsburgh, this additional nickname seemed quite fitting.

wafflewich: A waffle treat made by sandwiching a topping between two waffle halves or quarters.

woffelganger: Variation of "doppelganger." A waffle that looks exactly like your own, possibly because another waffle party attendee used exactly the same toppings as you did. Before accusing anyone of stealing your vegan waffle, make sure it's not just your woffelganger.

Wout!: Exclamation of excitement upon tasting the perfect waffle. It is a blend of "Woot!" and the last name of Cornelius Swartwout, who patented the first U.S. waffle iron on August 24, 1869.

Express Yourself

If you would like to help spread awareness about vegan food, consider hosting an event as part of the annual Global Vegan Waffle Party. Or, encourage your favorite local restaurant or other organization to sponsor one. See WaffleParty.com for additional details. There you'll also find inspirational photos and highlights from others' events, links to promotional materials including emailable posters and website logos, and other information to help spread the word. Never underestimate the awesome power of a delicious vegan waffle!

About the Author

Since 1998, Dave has baked waffles for the world's longest-running annual waffle party. The original house party has evolved into the Global Vegan Waffle Party, with individuals, organizations, and businesses hosting events worldwide. Through WaffleParty.com, Dave supports other hosts in spreading awareness about kinder, healthier, and more sustainable eating, and seeks their feedback on creating even better vegan parties and celebrations.

Dave also guides others to create happier and more powerful lives via his strategic life consulting business Idealist Coach (http://idealistcoach.com), and his self-empowerment guide for socially conscious people, *Naked Idealism*. He holds degrees in Psychology, Counseling, and Public Policy and Management, and is a Certified Life Coach. He has presented to various groups including the North American Vegetarian Society and American Mensa.

Dave enjoys composing dance music with social consciousness themes, beatboxing (creating rhythm and percussion with the mouth), gardening, hiking, and running in nature. He's completed a marathon and two half marathons since adopting a plant-based diet, and previously bicycled across the continent. He also has interests in promoting sustainable communities.

Dave skillfully removes a perfectly toasted vegan waffle.

Index

Agave nectar
  Carob Halvah Spread, 111
  Cocoa or Carob Agave Nectar, 103
All-purpose flour. *See* Flour, All-Purpose
Allspice
  Chai Spice Waffles, 65
  Creamy Spiced Apple Pie Sauce, 110
Almond
  -Amaranth Waffles, 66
  Anise Biscotti Waffles, 71
Amaranth flour. *See* Flour, amaranth
Amaretto
  Sauce, Amazing, 111
  Waffle Syrup, Dark Chocolate, 101
Amazing Amaretto Sauce, 111
Anise
  Biscotti Waffles, 71
Apple
  Pie Sauce, Creamy Spiced, 110
Apple cider
  Cider-Banana-Raisin Waffles, 62
  Cider-Pecan Waffles, 61
Applesauce
  Anise Biscotti Waffles, 71
  Crunchy Steel City Waffles, 48
  Pass the Buckwheat-Oat Waffles, 44
  PBMax (Peanut Butter to the Max)
    Waffles, 60
Avocado
  Cream, Raspberry, 107
  -Pecan Waffles for Two, 90
  Tool for mashing, 32
Awesome Samosa Waffles, Some, 95
Baby portabella mushrooms. *See*
  Mushrooms, baby portabella
Baking powder
  Leavener, as a, 25

Baking soda
  Leavener, as a, 25
Baking tips, 17–21. *See also*
  Troubleshooting baking problems
  Advance preparation of batter, 135–37
  Yeast-raised waffles, 21
Banana
  -Blueberry-Teff Waffles, 55
  Coco Kah-banana Syrup, 105
  -Fofana-Walnut Waffles, 80
  Mucho Molassesey Vegan Power
    Waffles, 97
  -Raisin Waffles, Cider-, 62
  -Spelt Waffles, Heartfelt, 45
  Tool for mashing, 32
Basil
  -Cornmeal Waffles, Orange-, 76
  -Orange Ice Cream, 114
  Sauce, Coconut-Cashew-, 118
  Southwestern Beans & Greens, 122
  Spicy Sloppy Tofu & Portabella, 124
  Umami Mama Waffles, 81
  You Make Miso Tangy Dipping Sauce
    (note), 119
Batter bowls
  Functions of, 32
Bean & Cornmeal Waffles, Refried, 78
Bean, Rice, & Cornmeal Waffles, Refried,
  79
Beans & Greens, Southwestern, 122
Beans, black
  Black Bean-Mango Tango, 121
  Refried Bean & Cornmeal Waffles, 78
  Refried Bean, Rice, & Cornmeal
    Waffles, 79
  Southwestern Beans & Greens, 122
Beans, pinto
  Southwestern Beans & Greens, 122

Binders, 26
  Substituting one for the other, 26
Biscotti
  Waffles, Anise, 71
Black beans. *See* Beans, black
Blackstrap molasses. *See* Molasses
Blueberry
  -Teff Waffles, Banana-, 55
Blue Tortilla Chip Waffles, Spicy, 73
Brown sugar
  Banana-Blueberry-Teff Waffles, 55
  Carrot-Ginger-Sage Waffles, 74
  Coconut-Date Waffles, 59
  Dark Chocolate Cake Waffles, 57
  Espresso-Maple-Walnut Syrup, 104
  Heartfelt Banana-Spelt Waffles, 45
  Kale-idoscopic Waffles, 88
  Naked Vegan Waffles, 37
  Nice Rice-Teff Waffles, 40
  Original Cinnamon-Raisin Waffles, 51
  Pass the Buckwheat-Oat Waffles, 44
  PBMax (Peanut Butter to the Max)
    Waffles, 60
  Spicy Sloppy Tofu & Portabella, 124
  Sweet Yeast-Raised Waffles, 43
  Textured Rice Waffles, 41
  Tropically Tanned Naked Waffles, 38
  Yeast-Raised Cinnamon-Raisin Waffles,
    52
  Yeast-Raised Cornmeal Chili-Dippin'
    Waffles, 91
  Yeast-Raised Waffles, 42
Buckwheat
  -Molasses Waffles, 47
  -Oat Waffles, Pass the, 44
  Waffles, Yeast-Raised, 46
Buckwheat flour. *See* Flour, buckwheat
Cake Waffles
  Dark Chocolate, 57
Canola oil. *See* Oils
Caramelized Onion & Garlic Waffles, 83

Cardamom
  Chai Spice Waffles, 65
  Creamy Maple-Chai Dream Sauce, 109
Carob
  Agave Nectar, 103
  Clumping, preventing, 34
  Cocoa, compared to, 29
  Crazeee Carob Syrup, 102
  Description of, 29
  Generously Ginger-Lemon-Chocolate
    Waffles, 54
  -Molasses Waffles, Cashew, 67
  Recipes using, 111
  Roasted versus raw powder, 29
  Syrup, Crazeee, 102
Carrot
  -Ginger-Sage Waffles, 74
  -Raisin Waffles, Spicy, 75
Cashew
  -Basil Sauce, Coconut-, 118
  -Carob-Molasses Waffles, 67
  Cinnamon Cream Cheese, 108
  Keen Zucchini-Dill Waffles, 94
  -Mushroom Sauce, Savory, 117
  Some Awesome Samosa Waffles, 95
  Waffles, Crispy Maple-, 56
Cashew butter
  Coconut-Cashew-Basil Sauce, 118
  Savory Cashew-Mushroom Sauce, 117
Cayenne
  Caramelized Onion & Garlic Waffles,
    83
  Chili-Lime Felafel Waffles, 85
  Hot Chocolate-Molasses Waffles, 58
  Kalamata Olive & Sun-dried Tomato
    Hummus, 128
  Kale-idoscopic Waffles, 88
  Mango-Chili Waffles, 69
  Mexican Chocolate Ice Cream, 112
  Mint Raita, 120
  Refried Bean & Cornmeal Waffles, 78

Refried Bean, Rice, & Cornmeal
  Waffles, 79
Southern Fried Tofu & Waffles, 126
South of the Border Dark Chocolate
  Syrup, 101
Southwestern Beans & Greens, 122
Spanakowafflita, 86
Spicy Blue Tortilla Chip Waffles, 73
Spicy Carrot-Raisin Waffles, 75
Spicy Sloppy Tofu & Portabella, 124
Umami Mama Waffles, 81
You Make Miso Tangy Dipping Sauce,
  119
Chai
  Dream Sauce, Creamy Maple-, 109
  Spice Waffles, 65
Cheddar Cheesy Waffles, 77
Cheesecakey Waffles
  Chocolate-Raspberry, 64
  Sinful, 63
Cheesy Waffles, Cheddar, 77
Cherry
  Almond-Amaranth Waffles, 66
Chickpeas
  Caramelized Onion & Garlic Waffles,
    85
  Kalamata Olive & Sun-dried Tomato
    Hummus, 128
Chili
  -Lime Felafel Waffles, 85
  Waffles, Mango-, 69
Chili-Dippin' Waffles
  Yeast-Raised Cornmeal, 91
Chili powder
  Black Bean-Mango Tango, 121
  Chili-Lime Felafel Waffles, 85
  Hot Chocolate-Molasses Waffles, 58
  Kalamata Olive & Sun-dried Tomato
    Hummus, 128
  Mango-Chili Waffles, 69
  Southwestern Beans & Greens, 122
  Spicy Sloppy Tofu & Portabella, 124

Chives
  Spicy Carrot-Raisin Waffles, 75
Chocolate
  Cake Waffles, Dark, 57
  Ice Cream, Mexican, 112
  -Molasses Waffles, Hot, 58
  Raspberry Cheesecakey Waffles, 64
  Syrup, Dark, 101
  Syrup, Dark Chocolate Amaretto, 101
  Syrup, Dark Chocolate Orangalicious,
    101
  Syrup, Dark Chocolate Peebee, 101
  Syrup, South of the Border Dark, 101
  Waffles, Generously-Ginger-Lemon, 54
Chocolate, dark. See Dark Chocolate
Chopsticks
  Removing waffles from iron with, 32
  Stirring yeast-raised batter with, 21, 32
Cider
  -Banana-Raisin Waffles, 62
  -Pecan Waffles, 61
Cider vinegar. See Vinegar, cider
Cilantro
  Black Bean-Mango Tango, 121
Cinnamon
  Banana-Blueberry-Teff Waffles, 55
  Banana-Fofana-Walnut Waffles, 80
  Carob Halvah Spread, 111
  -Carob Halvah Spread, 111
  Chai Spice Waffles, 65
  Cider-Banana-Raisin Waffles, 62
  Cider-Pecan Waffles, 61
  Cream Cheese, 108
  Creamy Maple-Chai Dream Sauce, 109
  Creamy Spiced Apple Pie Sauce, 110
  Crispy Maple-Cashew Waffles, 56
  Mexican Chocolate Ice Cream, 112
  Mucho Molassesey Vegan Power
    Waffles, 97
  Orange-Ginger Snap Waffles, 70
  Quinoa-Full Keen Waffles, 92
  -Raisin Waffles, Original, 51

-Raisin Waffles, Yeast-Raised, 52
Sinful Cheesecakey Waffles, 63
Sinfully Cinnamon Mapley Waffles, 39
South of the Border Dark Chocolate
    Syrup, 101
Clove
    Chai Spice Waffles, 65
    Creamy Maple-Chai Dream Sauce, 109
    Orange-Ginger Snap Waffles, 70
Cocoa. *See also* Cocoa powder
    Agave Nectar, 103
Cocoa powder
    Chocolate-Raspberry Cheesecakey
        Waffles, 64
    Clumping, preventing, 34
    Cocoa or Carob Agave Nectar, 103
    Dark Chocolate Cake Waffles, 57
    Dark Chocolate Syrup & Variations,
        101
    Hot Chocolate-Molasses Waffles, 58
    Mexican Chocolate Ice Cream, 112
Coco Kah-banana Syrup, 105
Coconut
    -Cashew-Basil Sauce, 118
    Coco Kah-banana Syrup, 105
    -Date Waffles, 59
    Ice Cream, Mango-Vanilla-, 113
    Very Coconutty Syrup, 106
Coconut milk
    Coco Kah-banana Syrup, 105
    Coconut-Cashew-Basil Sauce, 118
    Coconut-Date Waffles, 59
    Mango-Vanilla Ice Cream, 113
    Simple Piña Colada-ish Topping, 110
    Substituting for soymilk, 26
    Very Coconutty Syrup, 106
Coconutty Syrup, Very, 106
Coffee bean grinder. *See* Grinders
Coffee-flavored liqueur
    Coco Kah-banana Syrup, 105
Collard greens
    Southwestern Beans & Greens, 122

Cooking time, determining, 15–16
Coriander
    Chili-Lime Felafel Waffles, 85
    Some Awesome Samosa Waffles, 95
Cornmeal
    Chili-Dippin' Waffles, Yeast-Raised, 91
    Crispy Cornbuck Waffles, 49
    Description of, 23
    Southern Fried Tofu & Waffles, 126
    Spicy Blue Tortilla Chip Waffles, 73
    Waffles, Orange-Basil-, 76
    Waffles, Refried Bean, Rice, and, 79
    Waffles, Refried Bean and, 78
Cornstarch
    Southern Fried Tofu & Waffles, 126
Crazeee Carob Syrup, 102
Cream
    Raspberry-Avocado, 107
Cream Cheese
    Cinnamon, 108
Cream cheese, vegan, 29
    Chai Spice Waffles, 65
    Chocolate-Raspberry Cheesecakey
        Waffles, 64
    Sinful Cheesecakey Waffles, 63
Creamy Maple-Chai Dream Sauce, 109
Creamy Spiced Apple Pie Sauce, 110
Crispy Cornbuck Waffles, 49
Crispy Maple-Cashew Waffles, 56
Crunchy Steel City Waffles, 48
Cucumber
    Mint Raita, 120
Cumin
    Chili-Lime Felafel Waffles, 85
    Refried Bean & Cornmeal Waffles, 78
    Refried Bean, Rice, & Cornmeal
        Waffles, 79
    Southern Fried Tofu & Waffles, 126
    Southwestern Beans & Greens, 122
Dark Chocolate
    Amaretto Syrup, 101
    Cake Waffles, 57

Orangalicious Syrup, 101
Peebee Syrup, 101
Syrup, 101
Date
    Waffles, Coconut-, 59
Dill
    Keen Zucchini-Dill Waffles, 94
    Waffles, Keen Zucchini, 94
Ecological stewardship. *See* Environmental
    stewardship
Environmental stewardship
    At waffle parties, 144
Equipment for waffle making, 30–33
Espresso
    -Key Lime Waffles, 68
    -Maple-Walnut Syrup, 104
Felafel
    Waffles, Chili-Lime, 85
Flaxseed
    Banana-Fofana-Walnut Waffles, 80
    Binder, as a, 26
    Crispy Cornbuck Waffles, 49
    Grinding, 26
    Heartfelt Banana-Spelt Waffles, 45
    Kale-idoscopic Waffles, 88
    Pass the Buckwheat-Oat Waffles, 44
    Sesame Waffles, 98
    Spanakowafflita, 86
    Textured Rice Waffles, 41
    Umami Mama Waffles, 81
Flour, all-purpose
    Almond-Amaranth Waffles, 66
    Anise Biscotti Waffles, 71
    Avocado-Pecan Waffles for Two, 90
    Caramelized Onion & Garlic Waffles,
       83
    Carrot-Ginger-Sage Waffles, 74
    Chai Spice Waffles, 65
    Chili-Lime Felafel Waffles, 85
    Chocolate-Raspberry Cheesecakey
       Waffles, 64
    Cider-Pecan Waffles, 61

Dark Chocolate Cake Waffles, 57
Description of, 23
Espresso-Key Lime Waffles, 68
Kale-idoscopic Waffles, 88
Keen Zucchini-Dill Waffles, 94
Mango-Chili Waffles, 69
Naked Vegan Waffles, 37
Orange-Basil-Cornmeal Waffles, 76
Orange-Ginger Snap Waffles, 70
Original Cinnamon-Raisin Waffles, 51
Pass the Buckwheat-Oat Waffles, 44
PBMax (Peanut Butter to the Max)
    Waffles, 60
Sesame Waffles, 98
Sinful Cheesecakey Waffles, 63
Some Awesome Samosa Waffles, 95
Southern Fried Tofu & Waffles, 126
Spanakowafflita, 86
Spicy Blue Tortilla Chip Waffles, 73
Spicy Carrot-Raisin Waffles, 75
Sweet Yeast-Raised Waffles, 43
Tropically Tanned Naked Waffles, 38
Umami Mama Waffles, 81
Uses of, 23
Yeast-Raised Cinnamon-Raisin Waffles,
    52
Yeast-Raised Cornmeal Chili-Dippin'
    Waffles, 91
Yeast-Raised Waffles, 42
Flour, amaranth
    Almond-Amaranth Waffles, 66
    Description of, 23
Flour, buckwheat
    Buckwheat-Molasses Waffles, 47
    Crispy Cornbuck Waffles, 49
    Description of, 23
    Pass the Buckwheat-Oat Waffles, 44
    Uses of, 23
    Yeast-Raised Buckwheat Waffles, 46
Flour, oat. *See* Oats
Flour, quinoa. *See also* Quinoa
    Quinoa-Full Keen Waffles, 92

Flour, rice
    & Cornmeal Waffles, Refried Bean, 79
    Banana-Blueberry-Teff Waffles, 55
    Buckwheat-Molasses Waffles, 47
    Cashew-Carob-Molasses Waffles, 67
    Cider-Banana-Raisin Waffles, 62
    Coconut-Date Waffles, 59
    Crispy Cornbuck Waffles, 49
    Crunchy Steel City Waffles, 48
    Description of, 24
    Mapley Waffles, 39
    Mucho Molassesey Vegan Power
        Waffles, 97
    Nice Rice-Teff Waffles, 40
    Refried Bean, Rice, & Cornmeal
        Waffles, 79
    Textured Rice Waffles, 41
    Uses of, 24
    Yeast-Raised Buckwheat Waffles, 46
Flour, spelt
    Banana-Fofana-Walnut Waffles, 80
    Description of, 24–25
    Heartfelt Banana-Spelt Waffles, 45
    Uses of, 24–25
Flour, tapioca
    Buckwheat-Molasses Waffles, 47
    Cashew-Carob-Molasses Waffles, 67
    Cider-Banana-Raisin Waffles, 62
    Coconut-Date Waffles, 59
    Crispy Cornbuck Waffles, 49
    Crispy Maple-Cashew Waffles, 56
    Crunchy Steel City Waffles, 48
    Description of, 25
    Mapley Waffles, 39
    Mucho Molassesey Vegan Power
        Waffles, 97
    Nice Rice-Teff Waffles, 40
    Quinoa-Full Keen Waffles, 92
    Refried Bean, Rice, & Cornmeal
        Waffles, 79
    Textured Rice Waffles, 41
    Uses of, 25

Flour, teff
    Banana-Blueberry-Teff Waffles, 55
    Crispy Maple-Cashew Waffles, 56
    Description of, 25
    Nice Rice-Teff Waffles, 40
    Uses of, 25
Flour, whole wheat
    All-purpose flour, compared to, 25
    Anise Biscotti Waffles, 71
    Avocado-Pecan Waffles for Two, 90
    Caramelized Onion & Garlic Waffles,
        83
    Carrot-Ginger-Sage Waffles, 74
    Chili-Lime Felafel Waffles, 85
    Cider-Pecan Waffles, 61
    Dark Chocolate Cake Waffles, 57
    Description of, 25
    Espresso-Key Lime Waffles, 68
    Generously Ginger-Lemon-Chocolate
        Waffles, 54
    Hot Chocolate-Molasses Waffles, 58
    Kale-idoscopic Waffles, 88
    Keen Zucchini-Dill Waffles, 94
    Mango-Chili Waffles, 69
    Naked Vegan Waffles, 37
    Orange-Basil-Cornmeal Waffles, 77
    Orange-Ginger Snap Waffles, 70
    Original Cinnamon-Raisin Waffles, 51
    PBMax (Peanut Butter to the Max)
        Waffles, 60
    Refried Bean & Cornmeal Waffles, 78
    Sesame Waffles, 98
    Some Awesome Samosa Waffles, 95
    Spanakowafflita, 86
    Spicy Blue Tortilla Chip Waffles, 73
    Spicy Carrot-Raisin Waffles, 75
    Sweet Yeast-Raised Waffles, 43
    Tropically Tanned Naked Waffles, 38
    Umami Mama Waffles, 81
    Uses of, 25
    Varieties of, 25

Yeast-Raised Cinnamon-Raisin Waffles, 52

Yeast-Raised Cornmeal Chili-Dippin' Waffles, 91

Yeast-Raised Waffles, 42

Flour sifter, 34

Flours

Substituting, 22

Freeze & Squeeze Tofu

How to prepare, 125

Garam masala powder

Some Awesome Samosa Waffles, 95

Garbanzo beans

Chili-Lime Felafel Waffles. *See* Chickpeas

Garlic

Chili-Lime Felafel Waffles, 85

Kalamata Olive & Sun-dried Tomato Hummus, 128

Kale-idoscopic Waffles, 88

Savory Cashew-Mushroom Sauce, 117

Some Awesome Samosa Waffles, 95

Southwestern Beans & Greens, 122

Spanakowafflita, 86

Spicy Sloppy Tofu & Portabella, 124

Umami Mama Waffles, 81

Waffles, Caramelized Onion and, 83

Garlic powder

Orange-Basil-Cornmeal Waffles, 77

Southern Fried Tofu & Waffles, 126

Spicy Blue Tortilla Chip Waffles, 73

Generously Ginger-Lemon-Chocolate Waffles, 54

Ginger

Banana-Fofana-Walnut Waffles, 80

Chai Spice Waffles, 65

Creamy Maple-Chai Dream Sauce, 109

-Lemon-Chocolate Waffles, Generously, 54

-Sage Waffles, Carrot-, 74

Some Awesome Samosa Waffles, 95

Ginger, candied

Generously Ginger-Lemon-Chocolate Waffles, 54

Ginger Snap

Waffles, Orange-, 70

Global Vegan Waffle Party. *See also* Waffle party

Definition of, 148

History of, 132

Hosts & cities, 146–47

Ideas from other parties, 145

Participating in, 145, 148–49

World Vegan Waffle Day and, 132

Glossary of waffle vernacular, 148

Gluten

Binder, as a, 26

Gluten-free (GF) waffles

Banana-Blueberry-Teff Waffles, 55

Buckwheat-Molasses Waffles, 47

Cashew-Carob-Molasses Waffles, 67

Cider-Banana-Raisin Waffles, 62

Coconut-Date Waffles, 59

Crispy Cornbuck Waffles, 49

Crispy Maple-Cashew Waffles, 56

Crunchy Steel City Waffles, 48

Mapley Waffles, 39

Mucho Molassesey Vegan Power Waffles, 97

Nice Rice-Teff Waffles, 40

Refried Bean, Rice, & Cornmeal Waffles, 79

Textured Rice Waffles, 41

Yeast-Raised Buckwheat Waffles, 46

Granola

Espresso-Key Lime Waffles, 68

Graters

Functions of, 32–33

Types of, 32–33

Greens & Beans. *See* Southwestern Beans & Greens

Grinders

Functions of, 32–33

Types of, 32–33

Hempseed
Description of, 23
Mucho Molassesey Vegan Power
Waffles, 97
Uses of, 23

Hot Chocolate-Molasses Waffles, 58

Hummus
Kalamata Olive & Sun-dried Tomato,
128

Ice cream
Basil-Orange, 114
Mango-Vanilla, 113
Mango-Vanilla-Coconut, 113
Mexican Chocolate, 112

Ice cream maker, 33

Ingredient cards
For toppings at parties, 140

Kalamata Olive & Sun-dried Tomato
Hummus, 128

Kale-idoscopic Waffles, 88

Keen Waffles, Quinoa-Full, 92

Keen Zucchini-Dill Waffles, 94

Key Lime
Waffles, Espresso-, 68

Ladles
Functions of, 32

Leaveners, 25

Leftover waffles, reheating. *See* Reheating
waffles

Lemon
Chocolate Waffles, Generously-Ginger-,
54

Lemon juice
Carrot-Ginger-Sage Waffles, 74
Cinnamon Cream Cheese, 108
Espresso-Key Lime Waffles, 68
Kalamata Olive & Sun-dried Tomato
Hummus, 128
Lemon-Ginger Drizzle, 106
Orange-Basil-Cornmeal Waffles, 77
Raspberry-Avocado Cream, 107

Sesame Waffles, 98
Sinful Cheesecakey Waffles, 63
Some Awesome Samosa Waffles, 95
Spicy Carrot-Raisin Waffles, 75

Lime
Felafel Waffles, Chili-, 85
Mango-Chili Waffles, 69

Lime juice
Avocado-Pecan Waffles for Two, 90
Black Bean-Mango Tango, 121
Chili-Lime Felafel Waffles, 85
Chocolate-Raspberry Cheesecakey
Waffles, 64
Cilantro-Lime Tahini Sauce, 118
Coconut-Cashew-Basil Sauce, 118
Mango-Chili Waffles, 69
Refried Bean & Cornmeal Waffles, 78
Refried Bean, Rice, & Cornmeal
Waffles, 79
Spicy Blue Tortilla Chip Waffles, 73

Liquids, 26

Liquid smoke
Southwestern Beans & Greens, 122
Spicy Sloppy Tofu & Portabella, 124

Mango, 113
-Chili Waffles, 69
Tango, Black Bean-, 121
-Vanilla-Coconut Ice Cream, 113

Mango-Vanilla Ice Cream
-Vanilla Ice Cream, 113

Maple
-Cashew Waffles, Crispy, 56
-Chai Dream Sauce, Creamy, 109
-Walnut Syrup, Espresso-, 104

Maple syrup. *See* Syrup, maple

Mapley Waffles, 39
Sinfully Cinnamon, 39

Margarine. *See also* Oils
Cocoa or Carob Agave Nectar, 103
Crazeee Carob Syrup, 102
Creamy Spiced Apple Pie Sauce, 110

Dark Chocolate Syrup & Variations, 101

Espresso-Maple-Walnut Syrup, 104

Lemon-Ginger Drizzle, 106

Maple Syrup Supreme, 104

Mashers

Functions of, 32

Measurement of ingredients, 14–15

Batter, 15

Brown sugar, 15

Flour, 15

Green leafy vegetables & herbs, 15

"Packed" ingredients, 15

Mexican Chocolate Ice Cream, 112

Mint Raita, 120

Miso

Breaking up clumps with whisk, 32

Cheddar Cheesy Waffles, 77

Description of, 29

Spanakowafflita, 86

Umami Mama Waffles, 81

You Make Miso Tangy Dipping Sauce, 119

Mixing batter. *See* Stirring batter

Molasses

Buckwheat-Molasses Waffles, 47

Cashew-Carob-Molasses Waffles, 67

Cocoa or Carob Agave Nectar, 103

Crispy Cornbuck Waffles, 49

Crunchy Steel City Waffles, 48

Description of, 27

Hot Chocolate-Molasses Waffles, 58

Maple Syrup Supreme, 104

Mucho Molassesey Vegan Power Waffles, 97

Orange-Ginger Snap Waffles, 70

Spicy Sloppy Tofu & Portabella, 124

Tropically Tanned Naked Waffles, 38

Types of, 27

Waffles, Buckwheat-, 47

Waffles, Cashew-Carob-, 67

Waffles, Hot Chocolate-, 58

Yeast-Raised Buckwheat Waffles, 46

Yeast-Raised Cornmeal Chili-Dippin' Waffles, 91

Mother of Savory, The

Umami Mama Waffles, 81

Mucho Molassesey Vegan Power Waffles, 97

Mushroom

Sauce, Savory Cashew-, 117

Mushrooms, baby portabella

Savory Cashew-Mushroom Sauce, 117

Spicy Sloppy Tofu & Portabella, 122, 124

Mustard powder

Orange-Basil-Cornmeal Waffles, 77

Spicy Sloppy Tofu & Portabella, 124

Naked Vegan Waffles, 37

Naked Waffles, Tropically Tanned, 38

Name tags

For guests at parties, 140

Nice Rice-Teff Waffles, 40

Non-vegan dishes

Managing at parties, 139–40

Nutmeg

Avocado-Pecan Waffles for Two, 90

Banana-Fofana-Walnut Waffles, 80

Chai Spice Waffles, 65

Cider-Pecan Waffles, 61

Creamy Maple-Chai Dream Sauce, 109

Creamy Spiced Apple Pie Sauce, 110

Quinoa-Full Keen Waffles, 92

Nutmilks

Substituting for soymilk, 26

Nutritional yeast

Description of, 29

Kalamata Olive & Sun-dried Tomato Hummus, 128

Keen Zucchini-Dill Waffles, 94

Southern Fried Tofu & Waffles, 126

Southwestern Beans & Greens, 122

Spicy Blue Tortilla Chip Waffles, 73

Spicy Sloppy Tofu & Portabella, 124

Umami Mama Waffles, 81

Oats
Banana-Fofana-Walnut Waffles, 80
Crunchy Steel City Waffles, 48
Description of, 24
Forms of, including oat flour, 24
Orange-Basil-Cornmeal Waffles, 77
Original Cinnamon-Raisin Waffles, 51
Pass the Buckwheat-Oat Waffles, 44
PBMax (Peanut Butter to the Max)
    Waffles, 60
Uses of, 24
Yeast-Raised Cinnamon-Raisin Waffles,
    52

Oil, olive. *See also* Oils
Black Bean-Mango Tango, 121
Caramelized Onion & Garlic Waffles,
    83
Chili-Lime Felafel Waffles, 85
Southwestern Beans & Greens, 122
Spanakowafflita, 86
Spicy Carrot-Raisin Waffles, 75
Spicy Sloppy Tofu & Portabella, 124
Umami Mama Waffles, 81
You Make Miso Tangy Dipping Sauce,
    119

Oils, 28
Functions of, 28
Refillable spray bottles, 28
Spraying on waffle iron, 17–18, 28
Substituting, 28
Types of, 28

Olive. *See* Kalamata olive
Olive oil. *See* Oil, olive
Olives, Kalamata
Kalamata Olive & Sun-dried Tomato
    Hummus, 128
Umami Mama Waffles, 81

Onion
& Garlic Waffles, Caramelized, 83
Southwestern Beans & Greens, 122
Spicy Sloppy Tofu & Portabella, 124

Onion, green
Savory Cashew-Mushroom Sauce, 117
Spanakowafflita, 86

Onion powder
Chili-Lime Felafel Waffles, 85
Kale-idoscopic Waffles, 88
Orange-Basil-Cornmeal Waffles, 77
Refried Bean & Cornmeal Waffles, 78
Refried Bean, Rice, & Cornmeal
    Waffles, 79
Some Awesome Samosa Waffles, 95
Southern Fried Tofu & Waffles, 126
Spanakowafflita, 86
Spicy Blue Tortilla Chip Waffles, 73
Umami Mama Waffles, 81

Orange
-Basil-Cornmeal Waffles, 76
Dark Chocolate Orangalicious Syrup,
    101
-Ginger Snap Waffles, 70
Ice Cream, Basil-, 114

Orange, mandarin
Orange-Ginger Snap Waffles, 70

Orange extract
Basil-Orange Ice Cream, 114
Orange-Ginger Snap Waffles, 70

Orange juice
Orange-Basil-Cornmeal Waffles, 76

Oregano
Spicy Sloppy Tofu & Portabella, 124
Umami Mama Waffles, 81
You Make Miso Tangy Dipping Sauce,
    119

Original Cinnamon-Raisin Waffles, 51

Oven
Rising place for yeast-raised waffles, as
    a, 21

Paprika
Black Bean-Mango Tango, 121
Kalamata Olive & Sun-dried Tomato
    Hummus, 128
Mango-Chili Waffles, 69

Orange-Basil-Cornmeal Waffles, 77
Parsley
    Spanakowafflita, 86
Pass the Buckwheat-Oat Waffles, 44
PBMax Waffles, 60
Peanut butter
    Dark Chocolate Peebee Syrup, 101
    Kale-idoscopic Waffles, 88
    To the Max Waffles, 60
Peas
    Some Awesome Samosa Waffles, 95
Pecan
    Banana-Maple-Nut Syrup, 102
    Waffles, Cider-, 61
    Waffles for Two, Avocado-, 90
Pepper, black
    Caramelized Onion & Garlic Waffles,
        83
    Keen Zucchini-Dill Waffles, 94
    Southern Fried Tofu & Waffles, 126
    Southwestern Beans & Greens, 122
    Spicy Carrot-Raisin Waffles, 75
    Spicy Sloppy Tofu & Portabella, 124
    You Make Miso Tangy Dipping Sauce,
        119
Pepper, green
    Spicy Sloppy Tofu & Portabella, 124
Pineapple
    Simple Piña Colada-ish Topping, 110
Pinto beans. See Beans, pinto
Portabella
    Spicy Sloppy Tofu and, 124
Quinoa
    Description of, 24
    Forms of, including seeds & flour, 24
    -Full Keen Waffles, 92
Quinoa flour. See Flour, quinoa
Raisin
    Quinoa-Full Keen Waffles, 92
    Some Awesome Samosa Waffles, 95
    Waffles, Cider-Banana-, 62
    Waffles, Original Cinnamon-, 51

Waffles, Spicy Carrot-, 75
Waffles, Yeast-Raised Cinnamon-, 52
Raita, Mint, 120
Raspberry
    -Avocado Cream, 107
    Cheesecakey Waffles, Chocolate-, 64
Recycling
    At waffle parties, 144
Refried Bean & Cornmeal Waffles, 78
Reheating waffles, 19–20
Removing waffles from iron
    Using chopsticks, 32
Rice
    Waffles, Textured, 41
Rice flour. See Flour, rice
Rising yeast-raised batter, 21. See also Yeast-
    raised waffles
Safflower oil. See Oils
Sage
    Waffles, Carrot-Ginger-, 74
Samosa
    Waffles, Some Awesome, 95
Sauce
    Coconut-Cashew-Basil, 118
    Savory-Cashew Mushroom, 117
    You Make Miso Tangy Dipping, 119
Savory Cashew-Mushroom Sauce, 117
Sesame
    Waffles, 98
Sesame seed butter. See Tahini
Sesame seeds
    Sesame Waffles, 98
Sifter. See Flour sifter.
Sinful Cheesecakey Waffles, 63
Sloppy Joe. See Spicy Sloppy Tofu &
    Portabella
Sloppy Tofu & Portabella, Spicy, 124
Some Awesome Samosa Waffles, 95
Sour cream, vegan, 29
    Topping, as a, 72, 73, 78, 79
Southern Fried Tofu & Waffles, 126

South of the Border Dark Chocolate
    Syrup, 101
Southwestern Beans & Greens, 122
Southwestern Greens & Beans. *See*
    Southwestern Beans & Greens
Soymilk
    Substitutions, 26
Soy sauce
    Kale-idoscopic Waffles, 88
    Savory Cashew-Mushroom Sauce, 117
Spanakopita. *See* Spanakowafflita
Spanakowafflita, 86
Spatulas, 32
Spearmint leaves
    Mint Raita, 120
Spelt
    Waffles, Heartfelt Banana-, 45
Spelt flour. *See* Flour, spelt
Spiced Apple Pie Sauce, Creamy, 110
Spicy Blue Tortilla Chip Waffles, 73
Spicy Carrot-Raisin Waffles, 75
Spicy Sloppy Tofu & Portabella, 124
Spinach
    Spanakowafflita, 86
Spoons, 32
Steel City Waffles, Crunchy, 48
Stevia
    Substituting for other sweeteners, 28
Stirring batter
    How much to stir, 17, 32
    Yeast-raised batter, 17, 21
Strainer, wire mesh, 34
Sugar
    Description of, 27
    Types of, 27
Sun-dried tomato
    Hummus, Kalamata Olive and, 128
    Spicy Sloppy Tofu & Portabella, 124
    Umami Mama Waffles, 81
Sweeteners, 27–28
    Substituting, 27–28
Sweet Yeast-Raised Waffles, 43

Syrup
    Coco Kah-banana, 105
    Crazeee Carob, 102
    Dark Chocolate, & Variations, 101
    Dark Chocolate Amaretto, 101
    Dark Chocolate Orangalicious, 101
    Dark Chocolate Peebee, 101
    Espresso-Maple-Walnut, 104
    South of the Border Dark Chocolate,
        101
    Very Coconutty, 106
Syrup, maple
    Cinnamon Cream Cheese, 108
    Creamy Maple-Chai Dream Sauce, 109
    Crispy Cornbuck Waffles, 49
    Crispy Maple-Cashew Waffles, 56
    Description of, 27
    Espresso-Maple-Walnut Syrup, 104
    Maple Syrup Supreme, 104
    Mapley Waffles, 39
    Nice Rice-Teff Waffles, 40
    Original Cinnamon-Raisin Waffles, 51
    Quinoa-Full Keen Waffles, 92
    Sweet Yeast-Raised Waffles, 43
    Textured Rice Waffles, 41
    Yeast-Raised Cinnamon-Raisin Waffles,
        52
Tahini
    Carob Halvah Spread, 111
    Cilantro-Lime Tahini Sauce, 118
    Kalamata Olive & Sun-dried Tomato
        Hummus, 128
    Sesame Waffles, 98
Tapioca flour. *See* Flour, tapioca
Tapioca starch. *See* Flour, tapioca
Teff
    Waffles, Banana-Blueberry-, 55
    Waffles, Nice Rice-, 40
Teff flour. *See* Flour, teff
Teff grain
    Textured Rice Waffles, 41
Textured Rice Waffles, 41

Timers
    Functions of, 32–33
    Types of, 32–33
Tofu
    & Portabella, Spicy Sloppy, 124
    & Waffles, Southern Fried, 126
    Freeze & squeeze preparation method, 125
    Southern Fried Tofu & Waffles, 126
    Spicy Sloppy Tofu & Portabella, 124
Tofu & Waffles, Southern Fried, 126
Tofu, silken
    Cinnamon Cream Cheese, 108
    Creamy Maple-Chai Dream Sauce, 109
Tomato, crushed
    Southwestern Beans & Greens, 122
    Spicy Sloppy Tofu & Portabella, 124
Tomato, diced
    Southwestern Beans & Greens, 122
Tomato, sun-dried. *See* Sun-dried tomato
Tortilla Chip Waffles, Spicy Blue, 73
Tropically Tanned Naked Waffles, 38
Troubleshooting baking problems, 17–19
    Crispiness, lack of, 19
    Dry flour clumps, 17
    Dryness, 19
    Mushiness or softness, 19
    Rubbery waffles, 17
    Sticking to iron, 17–19
    Tough waffles, 17
Umami Mama Waffles, 81
Vanilla
    Ice Cream, Mango-, 113
Vegan guests
    Maintaining a safe environment for, 139–40
Veganism
    Reasons for being vegan, 10–13
Vegan Power Waffles, Mucho Molassesey, 97
Vegetable oil. *See* Oils
Very Coconutty Syrup, 106

Vinegar, balsamic
    You Make Miso Tangy Dipping Sauce, 119
Vinegar, cider
    Chai Spice Waffles, 65
    Spicy Sloppy Tofu & Portabella, 124
    Yeast-Raised Cinnamon-Raisin Waffles, 52
Vinegar, wine
    Spanakowafflita, 86
Waffle bakers. *See* Waffle irons
Waffle batter
    Advance preparation tips, 135–37
Waffle irons, 30–31
    Borrowing, 137
    Depth of waffle holes, 31
    "Done" light, 30
    Features of, 30–31
    Overflow catch tray, 31
    Purchasing on a limited budget, 31
    Rotating or flipping irons, 31
    Shape of waffles, 31
    Temperature control, manual, 30
    Timer with audio alarm, 30
    Used, 31
    Wattage, 30
Waffle makers. *See* Waffle irons
Waffle party. *See also* Global Vegan Waffle Party
    & Felafel Waffle tragedy, 20
    Advance preparation tips, 135–37
    Collaborating with other groups, 145
    Coordinating with other events, 145
    Definition of, 131
    Dietary requirements, managing, 140
    Diverse guest lifestyles, managing, 139–40
    Environmental stewardship at, 144
    Etiquette, 139–41
    Feedback from guests, receiving, 140–41
    Food preparation tips, 135–38

History of, 132

Hosting, 130–45

Large attendance, managing, 20, 134, 135–38

Mingling among guests, increasing, 140

Organizing, 130–45

Physical setting logistics, 142–43

Physical setup tips, dining room, 142

Physical setup tips, entryway, 142

Physical setup tips, kitchen, 142–43

Purpose of, identifying, 131–34

Reasons for throwing, 131

Requirements for, 131

Themes, 134

Vision for, developing, 132–34

Walnut

Banana-Maple-Nut Syrup, 102

Waffles, Banana-Fofana-, 80

Whisks, 32

World Vegan Waffle Day, 132

Xanthan gum powder

Banana-Blueberry-Teff Waffles, 55

Basil-Orange Ice Cream, 114

Binder, as a, 26

Buckwheat-Molasses Waffles, 47

Cashew-Carob-Molasses Waffles, 67

Chili-Lime Felafel Waffles, 85

Cider-Banana-Raisin Waffles, 62

Cider-Pecan Waffles, 61

Coconut-Date Waffles, 59

Crispy Maple-Cashew Waffles, 56

Crunchy Steel City Waffles, 48

Espresso-Key Lime Waffles, 68

Mango-Vanilla Ice Cream, 113

Mapley Waffles, 39

Mexican Chocolate Ice Cream, 112

Mucho Molassesey Vegan Power Waffles, 97

Nice Rice-Teff Waffles, 40

PBMax (Peanut Butter to the Max) Waffles, 60

Quinoa-Full Keen Waffles, 92

Refried Bean, Rice, & Cornmeal Waffles, 79

Spanakowafflita (note), 87

Yeast

Leavener, as a, 25

Yeast, nutritional. See Nutritional yeast

Yeast-raised waffles

Baking tips, 21

Caramelized Onion & Garlic Waffles, 83

Mixing tips, 21

Orange-Basil-Cornmeal Waffles, 76

Rising batter, 21

Sweet Yeast-Raised Waffles, 43

Umami Mama Waffles, 81

Yeast-Raised Cornmeal Chili-Dippin' Waffles, 91

Yeast-Raised waffles, 42

Yeast-Raised Buckwheat Waffles, 46

Yeast-Raised Cinnamon-Raisin Waffles, 52

Yogurt, soy

Almond-Amaranth Waffles, 66

Amazing Amaretto Sauce, 111

Banana-Blueberry-Teff Waffles, 55

Caramelized Onion & Garlic Waffles, 83

Cilantro-Lime Tahini Sauce, 118

Creamy Spiced Apple Pie Sauce, 110

Espresso-Maple-Walnut Syrup, 104

Mint Raita, 120

Savory Cashew-Mushroom Sauce, 117

Very Coconutty Syrup, 106

You Make Miso Tangy Dipping Sauce, 119

Zucchini

-Dill Waffles, Keen, 94